THE PERSISTENCE OF YOUTH

Recent Titles in
Contributions to the Study of World History

THE PERSISTENCE OF YOUTH

Oral Testimonies of the Holocaust

EDITED BY
Josey G. Fisher

Introduction by
Nora Levin

FROM THE HOLOCAUST ORAL HISTORY
ARCHIVE OF GRATZ COLLEGE

CONTRIBUTIONS TO THE STUDY OF WORLD HISTORY, NUMBER 32

GREENWOOD PRESS
NEW YORK • WESTPORT, CONNECTICUT • LONDON

Library of Congress Cataloging-in-Publication Data

The Persistence of youth : oral testimonies of the Holocaust / editor,
  Josey G. Fisher ; introduction by Nora Levin.
          p.   cm. — (Contributions to the study of world history, ISSN
  0885–9159 ; no. 32)
    "From the Holocaust Oral History Archive of Gratz College, Melrose
  Park, Pennsylvania 19126."
    ISBN: 0-313-28123-8 (alk. paper)
    1. Holocaust, Jewish (1939–1945)—Personal narratives.   2. Jewish
  children—Biography.   3. Oral biography.   I. Fisher, Josey G.
  II. Gratz College (Philadelphia, Pa.).   Holocaust Oral History
  Archive.   III. Series.
  D804.3.P48   1991
  940.53′18—dc20   89–27926

British Library Cataloguing in Publication Data is available.

Library of Congress Catalog Card Number: 89-27926
ISBN: 0-313-28123-8
ISSN: 0885-9159

First published in 1991

Greenwood Press, 88 Post Road West, Westport, CT 06881
An imprint of Greenwood Publishing Group, Inc.

Printed in the United States of America

The paper used in this book complies with the
Permanent Paper Standard issued by the National
Information Standards Organization (Z39.48-1984).

10   9   8   7   6   5   4   3   2   1

For the youth who grew up
and for those who never had the chance.

Contents

Preface

Memory, imperfect as it is, has its own reality. We block out certain thoughts. We cluster others. We telescope significant events to the exclusion of what seems insignificant. We incorporate details told to us by others and unknowingly they become our own. Past pain may be heightened; past pleasure may feel more precious, even poignant. However it is remembered, this is what happened. This is our history.

When we share our memory with someone, we may leave out certain details and stress others, depending on why we are telling our story, what we want the other person to know, or where their questions lead us. What we stress may depend on where we are in our lives, what day we choose to tell it, and who is listening.

The built-in fallibilities of oral history are also its strength. For the facts we have research. For the unique human experience we have memory.

In the ten years that we have been collecting over six hundred interviews of survivors for the Holocaust Oral History Archive of Gratz College, we have been impressed by the uniqueness of each story. While some may overlap in details, none duplicate in experience. Each person was caught in time, in the midst of his own distinct life, his path interrupted, his goals diverted. Each came to the years of crisis with his own personality, his strengths and weaknesses, his family and cultural tradition. We cannot speak in numbers. These voices on thousands of cassette tapes have nuances and pauses and perceptions that make each distinct and tell us that the voices which cannot be taped had been just as distinct, just as unique.

The youth of the Holocaust were caught in the time of their growing. Their external world had real enemies and unspeakable danger at the same time that their physical, psychological, and social development were propelling them toward adulthood. Internal intensity was intertwined with external threat, and their perceptions and responses reflect this. At the same time, these memories are viewed through the periscope of their adult years. Sometimes they parallel their memories with adult perspective. Sometimes they suspend the present as their eyes glaze, and they observe the sights of the past. Sometimes they re-enter that time frame, and their spare language reflects the sensations of childhood—the cold, the sounds, the fear.

Some feel that they missed their adolescence and were thrown precipitously from childhood into adulthood. Others describe that their dependence on their family was prolonged because of the war, others that romance and mature sexuality had to be postponed. Teenage life in Hitler's Europe was undoubtedly distorted together with the insanity of the time. What is remarkable is the persistence of the internal drive to grow up in a world without a future.

These fifteen stories cover a broad spectrum of youth. Some of the younger teenagers were caught in the Nazi web as children, their early self-image and sense of security affected by a climate of mockery, rejection, and fear. Others, already in their teens, were internally fortified by their early years with intact families and communities. Some lived out the war with their parents. Others were the only survivors of their immediate families. Within each personal circumstance and within each national experience in Nazi-controlled Europe, these young people continued to grow.

Adolescence is, by definition, a time of internal disequilibrium when the child struggles to become an individual, when he fluctuates between his ties to his parents and his new independence. He may shift his allegiance to a peer group or to a political, social, or religious organization that differs from his parents' interests while giving him support and a sense of independent action. Friends or group members may take on heightened importance and their opinions and acceptance become crucial to the young person's uncertain self-esteem. Parents' opinions and actions, on the other hand, are frequently criticized—not only as a way of affirming independent thought but also as an admission of fear and anger that the parents are not the all-perfect beings or the all-powerful protectors they were once thought to be.

Within these fifteen selections, the reader will see this ambivalence between dependence and independence. Such thoughts may not have been verbalized in the "children are to be seen and not heard" pattern of the early part of twentieth-century Europe but memory confirms the universality of these feelings. One child admires his father's bravery in the underground yet hints at his fear during the father's absences from the family and questions whether he, as a father, would have made the same choice. Others understood that their parents had strong national loyalties after centuries of residence in their homeland, yet could not understand their denial of the encroaching danger. From one description of parents as "not farsighted" to another castigating "the whole adult generation who let this happen," there is an interweaving of the internal struggle with the de-idealized parents, the larger de-idealized society, and the reality of painful decisions each person and each beloved parent had to make. But for some, they felt unprotected and very alone in their perception of reality. As one describes, it was "as if I were in a glass enclosure in a giant prison, and I could see everybody . . . but nobody could see me and I could not get out."

At the same time, the reader will observe the strong identification many of these young people had with their parents—a young German girl with her anti-Nazi father, a young Polish boy modeling his father's national pride, several channeling their ideals of adult strength through resistance and adaptive behavior in the camps. Some abruptly lost one or both of their parents and were thrown into adult roles with no transition; others protected parents in a sudden demand for role reversal; others watched in agony the slow physical and mental deterioration of their previously vital role models and protectors. Separation and individuation, for some of them, was not only an internal development; it was thrust upon them.

Attachment to a peer group that appears different from the parents' value system is another way of becoming independent. For instance, two girls from assimilated Jewish backgrounds upset their families when they become involved in Zionist youth organizations. A boy joined an underground resistance movement despite his parents' fears for his safety. These groups served as significant support systems reinforcing their developing identity. The boy states, "I don't think what we did made a hound's tooth of difference, but it made a big difference to me."

By the same token, rejection by the peer group is devastating at a time when acceptance is desperately needed. The young German girl was stigmatized by her classmates because she followed the anti-Nazi position of her family. Other children were rebuffed by significant friends whose parents either supported or feared Nazi condemnation. Some describe the humiliation of their socially unacceptable status, so painful when the peer group has such impact on self-esteem. As a result of the obsession with race in pre-war Nazi Germany, for instance, a young girl in Berlin and her Jewish classmates were told they would contaminate the other children and were physically separated, a withering message to an emerging self-image.

Concurrent with a normal spurt of physical development and a degree of internal confusion over the changes, Nazi-defined ''Jewish characteristics'' added complications. For some there was a degree of guilt if they ''passed'' as a non-Jew. Survival, however, sometimes depended on such camouflage. A Jewish boy finessed countless escapades and survived the war in a Romanian ghetto in part because he looked like a *Volksdeutsch*, of German descent. Yet it was painful to give that ''awful salute'' (*Heil* Hitler) to confirm his identity to Nazi soldiers. A Polish Jew lived out the war with Christian papers, her physical appearance blending with the non-Jewish community. Another teenager walked the streets of pre-war Berlin freely, appearing as a typical German schoolgirl. Yet the threat of physical attack from the classmates who knew her Jewish identity haunted her. To protect herself she became anonymous, copying the dress of the very girls she feared and masking her facial reactions. Others recount dreams that they had years later of their fear of physical attack.

Some of the teenagers describe fear, desperation, raw vulnerability. Others describe a protective numbness or relay terrifying incidents through a shield of factual narrative. What persists through each account is a degree of daring—from an insistant optimism in the face of deportations, to taking risks, to active aggression. For some, a smart remark to a policeman or an anti-Semitic civilian gave tremendous satisfaction. Others risked underground involvement with sabotage. For others, the drive to run and escape capture, to physically resist or retaliate, seemed instinctive. What was important was that they felt some sense of mastery, some degree of control, over an unpredictable and continually threatening existence. This drive to meet reality head on, the outward boldness of the internally shaking adolescent, no doubt accounted for many escapes and a sense of pride. The adolescent's discomfort with dependence and passivity coincided with historical reality and found its height of protest and resistance in the brave acts of these young people.

Issues of conscience frequently produce conflict during adolescence. Questioning of family values may be a way of looking independently at a moral code long taken for granted. Questioning societal values often points up hypocrisy, imperfection, or immorality in institutions or authority figures. During the Holocaust, young people faced an inclusively amoral system and struggled to establish a morality adaptive to their survival yet ethically comfortable. From lying to "liberating" camp food supplies, survival became the yardstick by which behavior was measured. Faced with "wrong" in the extreme, what was "right" became fluid and confusing. It was an exhilarating challenge to outwit the enemy or a quiet source of pride that they had not taken things "lying down." For some, small acts of vindication were enough; for others, retaliation and revenge for both personal and widespread atrocities were the only answer. Some could suspend their pre-war conscience during a time when morality was frequently absent. Others fought desperately to uphold morality as they had always known it.

With the intensification of Nazi persecution, the adolescent struggle against authority frequently transferred from struggle with parents to a very real, concretized enemy. As a result, what appeared to be age-typical conflicts with parents earlier in the Nazi period were replaced by apprehension about their fate, protectiveness, and, at times, unbearable feelings of loss. Guilt over what now seemed irrelevant past arguments ensued when there was no longer a chance to resolve tensions. Some of the younger adolescents struggled to protect their parents from their feelings of panic or despair, fearing that they would make things worse for them. Older adolescents sometimes assumed physically protective roles to their parents, describing their anguish at seeing them emaciated, heads shaven, physically or mentally debilitated. Some lived out the war years not knowing if their parents had survived; others experienced the devastation of their deaths. The difference between adult and child was blurred by the demands of history.

It is the vanished dream of joy, of light-hearted fun, of hope and plans for the future that these contributors speak of when referring to the loss of their youth. Incredibly, the internal struggles of their adolescence kept on going. Played out on a more demanding stage, growth intermixed with survival through mandatory coping and adaptive responses. Adolescence cannot be avoided; it is the necessary path to adulthood. But undoubtedly for some, facets of growing, much as facets of healing, had to be postponed until after the trauma of the war years.

One of the most frequently described delays was serious romantic involvement. We have reports of some group socialization—a dance with farm boys in Denmark, regular gatherings of young refugees in Uzbekistan, Zionist youth group meetings in Westerbork. In the midst of fleeing imprisonment in eastern Poland, one young man reports that he met a young lady and " . . . we used to go out together. Go out together? Where? There was nowhere to go." What appears to be most common is a delay of significant involvement until people were no longer starving and in life-threatening situations. "Who would have wanted to get married?" reflected one contributor. "You get so knocked down. The feeling is I am nobody. . . . I'm dead. . . . If you live a life like this, you don't care much about things." It was later that energy was freed to respond to emotional and sexual needs, and for some, the realization of the delay was painful: "I started thinking about myself [as a] little more than a machine who works and thinking about myself being a young woman . . . with needs . . . [and] having some kind of relationship. . . . What's going to be as far as my femininity is concerned?" Delayed but not diverted, several of these fifteen young people met their spouses at the end of the war or in displaced persons' camps and soon started their families.

It is now fifty years since the start of World War II, and its history is not yet complete. These oral testimonies give us a precious perspective— the process of living through that period. Through the prism of the present, the ongoing surge to grow up despite the horrors of the time are recalled with poignant, often painful honesty. These memories that reconstruct that experience bear testimony to the resiliance of the human spirit and the persistence of youth.

Josey G. Fisher, Assistant Director
Holocaust Oral History Archive
Gratz College
September 1, 1989

Acknowledgments

My selections for this anthology come from the Holocaust Oral History Archive of Gratz College, established in 1979 to record and preserve personal testimony of survivors of the Nazi period from 1933 to 1945. The extraordinary diversity of these accounts provides a multitude of perspectives from which to study this period, and it was within the specific theme of the adolescent experience that I selected and edited these histories.

My deepest gratitude goes to Nora Levin, founder of the Archive and Director until her death in 1989, for her unfailing support of this work and her thoughtful commentary on the manuscript. I wish to thank Lisa Tyre for reading an early draft and reinforcing my belief in the project, Lois Olena for her diligent processing of the text, and the Anna Bailis Foundation and Samuel S. Fels Fund for their important help. To my husband Fred and our children Joshua and Dara, my blessings and my love for being there.

My profound thanks goes to the fifteen people whose stories are recorded here, together with the hundreds of survivors who have shared their memories with us, bearing witness to their past and insuring that their testimony will instruct the future.

J.G.F.

Introduction

We hope that our anthology will be used not only to dramatize experiences of teenagers during the Holocaust, but also to arouse interest in the social and political dislocations in Europe following World War I which form the seedbed for the rise of fascism and Nazism. In Germany, these dislocations were particularly severe because of the shock and bitterness of a lost war, the widespread hunger, deprivation, and inflation that caused much suffering among the German people and made them susceptible to Nazi appeals. These appeals promised renewal of German national might, unity, and the elimination of so-called enemies, mainly Jews and Communists. Nazi propaganda became especially persuasive in the early thirties during a severe depression and during a period when the Weimar Republic failed to solve the serious economic, political, and social problems of German society. Yet, even after Hitler became chancellor in January 1933 and after the imprisonment of many Socialist and Communist candidates to the *Reichstag*, the Nazis received only 44 percent of the total votes in the last election on March 5, 1933. The Nazis had to destroy constitutional government before they could seize complete power.

Some understanding of the nazification of the German state, the introduction and spread of the apparatus of terror, and the specific anti-Jewish measures passed between 1933 and 1939 can help to deepen one's reading of Susan's story of her experiences in Germany before she emigrated in 1938. The experiences of David illuminate the dilemmas of parents and children involved in mixed marriages and expose the unending Nazi efforts to define Aryan racial purity. In the Wannsee Conference of January 20, 1942, when the Nazis officially decided on physical annihilation of European Jews as the "definitive solution of the Jewish problem," there was a very involved discussion of *Mischlinge* and Jews in mixed marriages. Tentatively, it was recommended that half-Jews be sterilized, but not deported, but these groups provided Nazi bureaucrats and racial "experts" with their most exasperating and, in the end, insoluble problems. In deporting such Jews, it was feared that "German blood" was being sacrificed. Arguments see-sawed back and forth and involved the German courts in balancing off the strengthening of German folkdom against the goal of eliminating all elements of possible Jewish contamination. Even during the savage fighting on the Russian front in 1942–43, Himmler's racial anthropologists were scouring the landscape searching for "Germanizable" people, including *Mischlinge* and Jews in mixed marriages.

The murder of Gypsies was somewhat selective, because Himmler considered some to have been descendants of the original Aryan race, and the racist ideologist Alfred Rosenberg was fascinated by them. However, many Nazis considered them alien, bearing dark and evil forces, and guilty of polluting German blood. Physical annihilation of Gypsies took place particularly in Germany or in German-controlled lands, especially in Poland. The testimony of Hans vividly describes the Nazi persecution of Gypsies.

Very soon after the Nazis came to power, all opposition was swiftly and ruthlessly eliminated. The very first prisoners in Dachau early in 1933 consisted of Communists; Socialists; labor leaders; and anti-Nazi editors, journalists, and writers. Soon thereafter the dread Storm Troops, Gestapo, and black-shirted SS police created terror throughout Germany and later, throughout German-occupied Europe. Every district in Germany was subdivided into small units with a block leader responsible for fifty households, keeping a dossier on each citizen and using a large network of informers to prevent the slightest criticism of the regime and to punish offenders. With the complete elimination of political and intellectual opposition, with the use of terror to instill fear and crush protest and render every individual mindlessly obedient, resistance in Germany was virtually non-existent. Anne Dore's family and others like it were extremely courageous in risking as much as they did.

Up to 1938, about 130,000 Jews had left Germany, some to Palestine, some to South America and Australia, and some to the United States. All had to have special permits and affidavits, which were difficult to obtain. A number also fled to countries in Europe which seemed to offer refuge such as France, Holland, and Czechoslovakia. However, when these countries were occupied by the Germans in 1940, German Jews were among the first to be sent to concentration camps and then deported to one of the death camps. The deportations were masked as "resettlements" in order to deceive the victims.

Westerbork, where Erica and her family from Germany were confined, was in Holland, at Assen, near the German border. It had originally been set up for Jewish refugees but became an assembly point for masses of Dutch Jews seized in raids. Despite Dutch resistance to the Nazis, including a general strike of Dutch workers in February 1941 to protest the seizure of 425 Jews who were deported to Buchenwald, and other expressions of Dutch solidarity, 115,000 Jews were deported, 100,000 to Auschwitz and Sobibor, and 15,000 to Theresienstadt in Czechoslovakia. At least 105,000 perished. Ernst, a native Dutch Jew, was, like Erica, deported to Westerbork, then Bergen-Belsen, and survived. Luck surely played a role, but their youth, too, made them hardier than older or very young Jews. Approximately 7,000 survived in hiding, protected by Dutch Christians who risked death, and, indeed, many of whom were fated to die for choosing to act out of conscience.

In Hanna's story, we find one of many instances of parents, unable to read the future, but desperately anxious to save their children, undergoing painful separations, while Hanna herself, as teenagers do, faced the future as an adventure. Her parents, like other Czech Jews, were suddenly shaken out of their comfortable lives in a liberal, democratic country in March 1939 when Czechoslovakia ceased to exist as an independent nation. Jews there were deported to the "Lublin Reservation" or to the ghetto of Terezin. More than 250,000 of 315,000 Czech Jews perished.

The most destructive consequences of the Nazi conquest of Europe for Jews took place in Poland, where over three million perished in the ghettos and deportations. All of the death camps were in Poland, so that, additionally, most of the other three million Jews who died passed through Poland. Despite widespread Polish anti-Semitism, some Poles risked their lives to hide Jews or procure false papers for them. Lili's experiences describe the predicaments felt on both sides.

Polish Christians also suffered greatly under the Nazis, for they, too, were considered "subhumans" and "disposable," except to serve Germans as laborers. Many Polish clergy, intellectuals, and aristocrats were executed early during the Nazi occupation. Old conflicts between Poles and Ukrainians in Poland erupted and form a large part of Marian's story.

Henry's suffering in Nazi camps and ghettos in Poland was duplicated many times over in the lives of hundreds of thousands of victims. Fortunately, Henry was one of the lucky ones who survived. Very few did.

The experiences of Chayale, Myer, and Isadore can be understood against the changing map of Eastern Europe after the German invasion of Poland in September 1939 and after the German invasion of the Soviet Union in June 1941. From September 1939 to June 1941, all people, including Jews in eastern Poland, the Baltic states, and Bessarabia, were subject to Soviet control and destruction of traditional economic, religious, and cultural life. Those who refused to accept Soviet citizenship were deported to Siberia under inhumane conditions and struggled to survive in strange, often primitive communities, or in isolation. After the German invasion of the Soviet Union, all Jews, Gypsies, Soviet commissars, and "socials" previously under Soviet control were marked for murder by mobile killing squads called *Einsatzgruppen*, who accompanied the German army and which were instructed to carry out planned mass executions. Altogether, four *Einsatzgruppen* of battalion strength were set up: Group A in the Baltic states, Group B in White Russia, Group C in the Ukraine, and Group D in the Crimea-Caucasus. Each group consisted of from 500 to 900 men, many coming from the ranks of the German Security Police and Waffen SS, from pools of motorcycle riders, teletype and radio operators, and clerks. Indigenous units of Ukrainians, Latvians, Lithuanians, and Estonians were added as auxiliary police when numbers had to be filled out. At their training centers at Pretsch in Saxony, the men became expert marksmen and listened to lectures and speeches on the necessity of exterminating subhumans threatening the life of Germany.

Jews in the Soviet Union were particularly vulnerable to the Nazi invaders. Older Jews remembered the benign German occupation of western Russia during World War I, and because the Nazi-Soviet Pact of August 1939 (which gave eastern Poland and the Baltic states to the Soviet Union) did not permit any information about the Nazi persecution of Jews elsewhere to be made known to Soviet Jews, they were not at all prepared for the Nazi assault. Some even believed the German army was coming as a liberation army.

The story of Samuel, born in Lithuania, and that of Nathan, born in Romania, both dramatize the uprooting and perils in the sudden shifting tides of war as the Nazis conquered previously held Soviet territory and as the youths struggled to survive without any anchors—family, home, political, or institutional support.

Where, then, it is often asked, was Jewish resistance? Despite Nazi-controlled conditions, there was much more than is popularly known, including physical, armed resistance in many ghettos, forests, and even in the death camps, generally organized by youths. There was also much passive resistance, involving sabotage, and clandestine educational, cultural, and religious activity, which was forbidden by the Nazis. The conditions facing Jews in Nazi Europe had no precedents to guide them and, as can be understood from the accounts in the anthology, doomed any and all resistance efforts. The Nazis cleverly concealed their intentions to murder all Jews while, at the same time, they forced Jews to use their diminishing energy to battle hunger, disease, shock, slave labor, debasement, and hopelessness. Moreover, in contrast with non-Jewish resistance, Jews had no national home, no national army, no national leadership or source of allied help. Many thousands of Jews fought in Soviet, Polish, French, and Dutch fighting forces, but their identity has been concealed.

The stories of Jewish youths in this anthology also reveal the great diversity of Jewish life in Europe and the variety of European cultures in which they lived before the war. Once under Nazi control, they were forcibly separated, unable to communicate with each other or to unite. Moreover, they did not face the Nazi so-called Final Solution at the same time. The pace of destruction varied from country to country, while the tide of victory for the Allies in 1943–44 intensified, instead of diminished, the deportations and killings.

These youthful testimonies cannot avoid the savagery and horror of the Holocaust, but we must not linger there. Young adults in America can reflect on the dilemmas and moral choices their counterparts in Europe experienced fifty years ago and examine their own values and deepest core of character. In that process, perhaps the readings will help to strengthen democratic and humanitarian attitudes and behavior for a new generation.

Nora Levin, Director
Holocaust Oral History Archive,
Gratz College
August 1, 1989

The Partition of Poland, September 1939

FINLAND
Vyborg
Helsinki
GULF of FINLAND
Leningrad
Moscow
Tallin
ESTONIA
BALTIC SEA
Riga
LATVIA
LITHUANIA
Danzig
Kovno
Vilna
EAST PRUSSIA
U. S. S. R.
Grodno
Minsk
Białystok
Lodz
Warsaw
POLAND
Lublin
GENERAL GOVERNMENT
Kiev
Crakow
Zhitomir
GREATER GERMANY
Lvov
BUKOVINA
PROTECTORATE of BOHEMIA and MORAVIA
SLOVAKIA
BESSARABIA
Kishinev
AUSTRIA
Vienna
HUNGARY
Odessa
ROMANIA
BLACK SEA

▓ SOVIET ANNEXATIONS, 1939-40

Poland Under German Rule After June 22, 1941

German Occupation of U.S.S.R., June 22, 1941–42

REICHSKOMMISSARIAT
OSTLAND — Leningrad

Baltic Sea

ESTONIA

Riga
LATVIA   Einsatzgruppe A

GERMANY   LITHUANIA

                          Smolensk   Moscow
BIALYSTOK
DISTRICT   WHITE
              RUSSIAN   Einsatzgruppe B
Warsaw   S.S.R   Minsk
Slonim
          Volhynia – Podolia
GOVERNMENT   Einsatzgruppe C   Kursk
GENERAL   Rovno   Kiev
                Lvov   REICHSKOMMISSARIAT
                        UKRAINE   Stalingrad
HUNGARY

Arad   Cluj
            Jassy   Einsatzgruppe D
BESSARABIA   Rostov
                            Sea
                            of
TRANSNISTRIA   ROMANIA   Azov
            Bucharest   Odessa
BULGARIA Istanbul Black Sea CRIMEA
            Constanza   Simferopol
                        TURKEY

U. S. S. R.

Legend:
—×— Extent of German Advance
– – – Western Boundary, U.S.S.R.,
       Prior to June 22, 1941

Axis Europe, 1942

1   *Susan*

Susan describes in poignant detail her teenage years in Nazi Germany before her family left for Guatemala in 1938. Intimidated and mocked by teachers and classmates, Susan cherished the courageous support of a significant few. Vulnerable, frightened, and criticially aware of the encroaching danger, she was dependent on an adult world that seemed to minimize or even deny their precarious position.

German Jews found themselves increasingly restricted and shunned by Nazi measures. By 1938, German Jews were no longer citizens. They had no civil rights or political rights. Jewish artists and professionals could not work for non-Jews; Jewish-owned businesses were "Aryanized" (taken over by German owners). Jewish children were removed from public schools and segregated in Jewish schools. Jews were forbidden to mix with Germans in public parks, places of entertainment, and stores.

Because of the very limited number of places to which they could emigrate, by the end of 1937 only one-fourth of the German Jews had left Germany. Many, like Susan's father, were patriotic Germans—veterans of World War I, who identified with their country's culture and history— who still hoped the Nazi restrictions were temporary and viewed emigration as causing unnecessary social and economic upheaval. Others who wanted to leave, especially by 1938, were restricted by procedural red tape and inflexible immigration quotas of other countries. Approximately ninety percent of those Jews who were unable to leave perished.

Born to an upper-middle-class Jewish banking family in Berlin in 1921, Susan experienced both the strict mode of child rearing—such as eating

everything on her plate or being served the same food for her next meal—
as well as the liberal culture of the salons of pre-war Berlin. Her father
kept the Iron Cross awarded him for his service in the First World War
in a paperweight on his desk, but the family's religious identification was
less specific.

My father was, I guess you might call, a humanistic Jew. . . . He took me to
Yom Kippur services one time. . . . We did celebrate Christmas at home with
Christmas tree and all . . . and it never occurred to me to question any of this.
. . . The friends that we had also had that same kind of totally assimilated attitude
and so there was no note of incongruity as I was growing up.

I do remember, somehow though, that when I was in perhaps second grade,
during the Advent season in public school, that each day prior to Christmas,
one girl from the class would be chosen to open another window in a little Advent
card. . . . I remember thinking at the time that there was something for me [that
was] unhappy . . . that I was forced to sit there and participate in a majority ritual
without actually being a part of it.

Despite being a shy and somewhat fearful child, Susan found great
release in a gymnastics class which she attended from the time she was
two. It was run by a retired army major.

I quickly became the star of this class and when he was asked to participate in
a famous health cult movie . . . in 1925 . . . "Ways to Strength and Beauty," our
class participated in that movie and I was the only one of whom a close-up shot
was made. My father took me to every performance and I remember seeing
myself up there on the screen at age four running into the camera with an
extremely happy face. . . . Even though I knew that my parents could no longer
afford it [after the financial crash of 1928] . . . the major had said that he could
let me come for free because . . . he loved me so much and because I had been
there for so many years and he felt that I could be useful to demonstrate the
exercises to the other children. . . . At one point shortly after the Nazis came to
power . . . the major . . . had come up to me and had said with tears in his eyes
that I could no longer come back to his class. He was, of course, not allowed
to have me in his class anymore and I always felt that he was one of the very
few people that I considered as . . . humane and decent.

For a while during Susan's childhood, the family continued to prosper
financially.

We had a Mercedes Benz and we had even a chauffeur. . . . And the chauffeur
would bring me . . . to the gym class, but I was so embarrassed about being so

singled out from the other girls in the class, that I pleaded with him to . . . wait for me two blocks away from the school so that the other girls wouldn't see him. . . . What seemed like an idyllic life, however, came to a very abrupt end.

With the 1928 economic crash came a sharp change in the family's life. Ongoing problems now resulted in her parents' divorce. Her father lost his position at the bank. Her mother started to work and moved with Susan and her younger sister to a modest apartment. At first, Susan was unaware of the real impact of the change.

Life, in fact, for me became a little better now because for the first time I felt that I was useful. I was called upon to . . . help with dishes . . . with marketing . . . to take my little sister to the dentist or to the nursery school. . . . I was not yet ten years old then and I was extremely proud of this new found authority and of the fact that I was being trusted.

Political developments began around 1929 in Berlin . . . to turn ugly in certain ways. . . . The whole question of Jewishness somehow began in some fashion that I am not quite sure of . . . but there must have been something in the air. . . . This [was also the] beginning of a consciousness of [my] Jewish identity. . . . If I remember correctly, it came through relatives in Hamburg who were . . . quite Zionist. . . . One of my cousins . . . began to argue with me and . . . somehow there was this beginning of consciousness that we were Jews and . . . I should be aware of this. But . . . I always was reluctant to talk about this to my parents.

[Also] when I was about ten, I began to develop more of an interest on my own. I was reading enormously. . . . My horizons began to widen and I began to be more aware of my surroundings. . . . I now began to look at newspapers, headlines, and especially . . . the round *kiosks* at the corner of the streets where the announcements were made for the cultural events . . . political meetings . . . proclamations. . . . It was really, in a sense . . . a very good overview of the cultural and political situation of the day . . . and I began to see in around 1931 that the political situation was heating up.

Although Susan's family was suffering financial reversals during the Depression,

we were totally unaware [of the extent] of the economic hardships that were so current in other parts of Berlin. . . . We were totally insulated and even in the public school that I was going to . . . there were few working class girls. . . . I do recall our . . . housekeeper . . . saying to us that when she was fourteen she had gone into service as a maid and had saved and scrimped for several years to put a little bit of money into a savings account and that, one day during the terrible . . . inflationary period in the early '20's, she had taken her entire savings and had bought one loaf of bread with it. . . . I had a sense from a certain bitter tone on her part that she still had much resentment. . . . I also know . . . from later on, that she had great bitterness against my father. . . . My father had been a Social Democrat, as had everyone else in the family, but somehow or other, as he had become more prosperous, he supposedly abandoned his earlier principles and became a typical *nouveau riche*. . . . I cannot ever say that [she] was anti-Semitic . . . but I do feel . . . that she associated the excesses or the [upper middle class lifestyle] of my father with the fact that he was Jewish.

Susan now became much more aware that this attitude reflected a larger anti-Semitic scene.

I would see posters . . . horrendous caricatures. . . . At first when I saw it, it filled me with real loathing and also tremendous anxiety. I was not quite sure how to cope with it. . . . I did not know how to counter the growing anti-Semitic propaganda and the caricatures and the attacks made on Jews on many fronts, because I had so little positive identification as a Jew from my own background and experience.

Grade school for Susan had been relatively problem-free, but high school, starting in the early 1930's, paralleled the conflicts that were growing throughout Germany.

I made friends with a young girl named Christa . . . with blonde braids and porcelain blue eyes . . . really not a very nice person, but for some unknown reason, she had taken a liking to me. . . . Her father was a railroad clerk and . . . they were working class people. . . . She would come over to our house for dinner quite frequently . . . on picnics . . . to a café for my beloved *apfelkuchen*, apple cake with whipped cream . . . and so she shared in a lot of the goodies that my parents were very generously offering because they, too, were happy that I had a friend. . . . I was happy to be noticed. I had not had any friends before, so for me this was a marvelous thrill. And, also, there was the additional fact that she was blonde and had blue eyes and I had so wanted blonde braids and here I was with my wispy brown hair. . . . I thought that the blonde with blue eyes was, after all, much more normal . . . and why did I have to be different? And I admired her for looking like everybody else, and I guess that was one reason why I took to her. . . . I was so happy at finding somebody who didn't seem to be unusually intelligent and didn't stand out because of the intelligence. She was just like everybody else, and I guess that's what I wanted her to be.

Then in November of '32, when Hitler first won his first partial election . . . Christa came up to me and in front of everybody during recess . . . said in a loud voice, . . . "I can't be friends with you anymore. . . . My father does not want me to be friends with a Jew,'' and then she just looked at me with those cold blue eyes. . . . I was so overwhelmed with horror and with rage. . . . I just felt that I was going to choke. My emotions were coming up into my head. I could hardly breathe but I couldn't say anything. I could see that everybody was watching and listening. And [I was filled with] shame and embarrassment over having her say this in front of everyone to begin with and also the sense that she had absolutely not the slightest feeling of compunction about it. . . . I was then eleven and a half.

For the next five years, Susan and her family struggled with the increasing anti-Jewish restrictions. But during the 1930's,

as far as I was concerned, [the impact] was really much more psychological than it was physical. . . . Obviously there were many restrictions on our lives . . . but, on the whole, it was the psychological effect that was really indelible.

[Because] I had never developed a positive Jewish image, I found it so terribly difficult to respond to any attacks that were directed against me or against the Jewish people in my presence. I did not know . . . what was true and what was false.

Many times . . . the girls in school would leave a copy [of] *Die Stürmer* . . . the infamous hate sheet put out by Julius Streicher daily—on my desk during recess. . . . I didn't know what to do with it. . . . What I usually did was just put it under the desk. . . . There was this tremendous fear . . . of any kind of physical confrontation. . . . In spite of my being an excellent gymnast and being an excellent athlete, in many ways I was just terrified of being beaten up and I knew that there were occasions when the Hitler-Jugend or boys in the Hitler Youth were beating up Jewish kids. And at that time the BDM, in other words, the League of German Girls . . . were also now proliferating in the school . . . and many of them were much taller and much stronger than I. And I was not a quick runner, so I was always afraid of being caught.

One reason this did not materialize was because I learned how to make myself inconspicuous. This became my great defense. . . . I learned to melt into the landscape. I wore my hair short and I wore basically the same clothes as the other girls . . . no make-up, ankle socks . . . oxford shoes . . . skirts and blouses as did the others [and] a tweed jacket that . . . in its outline was very similar to . . . the uniforms . . . of the other girls.

I happened to be blessed with being farsighted, so when I would walk down the street I could look ahead to the end of the block. . . . If I saw a group of uniformed kids . . . I would very quietly cross the street. . . . It became almost a second nature to me to look out for danger. . . . From the time that Hitler came to power, I would say that there was not a day that I did not walk to school or walk back from school without a sense of fear in the pit of my stomach. . . . It was clear that this was not simply an irrational fear on my part. These things were going on.

[In] 1933 we were separated in the classroom. . . . We had to sit in front of the classroom so that we would not "contaminate" the Aryan children. . . . Once a week we had to go to the auditorium to listen to a propaganda speech over the radio, usually by Hitler, and we had to sit on the back bench . . . totally separated from the rest of the girls. But we had to attend. There was no way for us to get out of it. And each time when the speaker would say something against the Jew . . . the entire school almost would turn around and look at . . . our faces to see our reactions. The strength of will and of nervous energy that it took for me to make my face into a total poker face during those times . . . became a habit which unfortunately . . . remained for me . . . at times of extreme stress and extreme anger and extreme pain . . . for many years to come.

Ever conscious of not giving these classmates cause for anger, Susan whispered an answer during class when a girl asked her for a history date.

I was afraid not to give them these answers. . . . The teacher [who had taught] my mother and her younger sisters . . . [who] knew the family . . . said, "Keep your mouth shut. You are merely a guest in this country," . . . presumably to curry favor with the girls in the classroom or to show what a marvelous patriotic Nazi and German he was. . . . I was absolutely beside myself with anger and rage, [but] I just could not talk to anybody about it, and I was up the entire night and all I could think of was, "Why didn't I say something back to him? Why didn't I walk out? . . . Why didn't I defend myself?" . . . I was enraged by the fact that there was nothing I could do, and the sense of this powerlessness became so overwhelming that it was something that stayed with me for a long time.

It was terrifying to Susan to see an adult equally intimidated by these girls.

A physics teacher [who] was Jewish . . . an older man [who] had a shaking of some sort, probably from his injuries [when] he had been shell-shocked in the First World War . . . came into our class and what the girls in our class did to make that man miserable cannot be described. . . . They would put gum in his chair, they would throw catapults at him, they would start screaming, they would throw papers. . . . The man would stand up there shaking like a leaf with fear and with suppressed rage and with impotence. . . . I saw the sadism and the brutality among these young women and how they enjoyed torturing and tormenting this poor man and it was just really beyond belief to see the pleasure with which they saw him suffer.

Susan could recall several displays of humanity as well.

There were very few people that openly dared to help Jews or side with us
. . . [but] there were some . . . few incidents where there was some integrity. . . .
In my composition class in German in public school, [when] I was about thirteen,
the teacher had asked us to do a book review about three favorite authors, and
she specified that they must all be German and, of course, me being a rebel, I
refused to listen to this. . . . She had no hesitancy about my reading my reviews
of two non-Germans and one German authors, which I thought was relatively
courageous in those days, at a time when courage was really measured in some
very small acts of personal integrity.

I also had my gym teacher who was very fond of me. . . . In the sixth grade,
I believe, I won first prize in a national gymnastics contest for my grade, but
she called me over and she said to me, "Now, Susan, you know that I can't
give you the prize because if the judges would know that a non-Aryan had won
in gymnastics they would be terribly upset and angry at me. . . ." She was
almost in tears at having to hurt me so much, but in fact, I didn't care. To me
the whole thing was absolutely ludicrous. I knew that I had won, I knew that
the girls knew that I had won, which to me was even more important, and I
knew she knew it, and that was all I cared about. I certainly was not interested
in advancing the cause of gymnastics in Nazi Germany.

There was a young girl in my class who was the only Catholic. She was from
the working class. . . . She was the only one who was kind and talked to me . . .
because she herself was also ostracized because she was a Catholic and . . .
working class and she would have to leave the school at age fourteen. . . . There
was a certain bond between both of us being sort of socially unacceptable, and
I appreciated that.

During this same time, Susan experienced her most significant en-
counter with Jewish identity.

The one thing that I might say that was positive, if there is such a thing, about
the Hitler movement, was the fact that for the first year after the Nazis came to
power there was religious instruction in the schools, including even Jewish
instruction . . . for one hour a week. And each time when we left the classroom,
there was general tittering and even loud derision on the part of the Christian
girls, but somehow it didn't seem to bother me particularly because I enjoyed
the Jewish instruction. We had a marvelous teacher [Rabbi Regina Jonas]. She
was an ordained rabbi who was unable to get a [pulpit] because of being a
woman, and I have a feeling that she was really a feminist. . . . I always thought
of her as being sort of a Biblical matriarch like Rebecca from the Bible. She
was rather an imposing figure and quite handsome [with] beautiful black hair
that she had braided around her head. . . . I immediately was carried away by

the beauty of the Old Testament and I read the entire Bible. . . . She was very proud of me. I was one of her prize pupils.

That year we had a Chanukah play. . . . I was one of the candles, supposedly of a menorah, and we all had a verse that we had to recite in Hebrew and it was a very exciting thing to me. . . . But this instruction was terminated at the end of that first year.

As time went on . . . some of the Jewish girls were disappearing and going into private Jewish schools. It never occurred to me to ask.

Other problems were developing. Among them, should we say, "*Heil* Hitler" as the teacher walked in every morning? The feeling was finally that for Jews to say, "*Heil* Hitler," would be a desecration of the holy Aryan alliance or whatever, and we were then excused, but . . . it was always a frightening moment . . . to stand there and have everybody around me salute. . . . There was always that one minute when I was expecting some kind of repercussion that never happened.

The atmosphere . . . became very oppressive. . . . We were developing a sort of subterranean network among the Jews in Berlin. We all had the impression . . . which I think was fostered deliberately by the Nazis that our phones were tapped, that our mail was read, and that there was just no way that we could communicate without being overheard and that every communication was in some way dangerous. When we wanted to say anything, we would walk into the bathroom, pull the shades down, and turn the water on full force and then we would whisper and the impression was that each janitor or superintendent of each building was a member of a . . . Nazi cell. . . . It may well have been true but we had no evidence.

The whole life just became very circumscribed. . . . I was becoming more and more isolated. . . . And yet . . . I kept on walking the streets of Berlin. It was the only way I felt that I could be part of this society and also . . . it was a self-protective device in the sense that I could keep acquainted with the changing atmosphere . . . as a sort of alarm system . . . so that I could be prepared for myself and my family. In many ways I had a great sense of what was going on because of the very fact that in the school, the girls . . . the classroom and the teachers . . . mirrored the prevailing atmosphere outside.

[I was] compulsively listening to the radio. . . . I fixed our radio in such a way that I could receive shortwave. I knew this was a capital offense and I used to turn the speaker . . . way down and put a blanket over the radio and then put my ear right against the speaker so that I could hear news broadcasts. . . . And once, late at night . . . I heard a Salzburg festival broadcast . . . and to me that was the green oasis of our existence at that time. . . . On occasion, I would sneak into a movie [or] use public transportation . . . because I did not "look" Jewish. . . . I could do a lot of things that possibly some other people might not have been able to do. . . . I looked inconspicuous like any German girl maybe from Silesia. . . . In a sense, it almost made me feel guilty. I felt that I was getting away with something I might not have if I had looked more typically Jewish.

Susan's sense of the Nazi threat sharpened when the Nuremberg Laws were put into effect in 1935.

The sense of total omnipotence that the Nazis had created came home to me. . . . I was . . . going through the streets . . . and Hitler was passing. . . . There was a storm trooper standing almost directly in front of me and in his holster he had a large pistol and I thought, "What would happen if I would grab his pistol and run like mad towards where Hitler was passing and try to kill him?" I realized that this was totally irrational. . . . Yet it was almost like a compulsion for me to think about it and fantasize. . . . I had . . . the early adolescent messianic idea, I guess, that I was going to lead my people out of bondage . . . [that] sense of needing to be a hero and feeling yourself omnipotent. . . . I was not worried about being killed . . . but the one thing that stopped me, aside from all the other considerations, was the fear that they would then get a hold of my [family] and that they would be tortured.

Susan was incensed when her father, who had been divorced from her mother for seven years, refused an opportunity in 1936 to emigrate to England. Her pleas for him to leave proved useless. He was a war veteran with an Iron Cross, he told her. The Germans would not harm him.

I could not believe that he could be so blind and that he could really fool himself like that. . . . I said, "But they don't care any more about these things. . . . Doesn't it look like it's a very frightening situation? . . . Don't you see the danger?" . . . He told me at the time, "Well, after all, Hitler did do some good things and look, at least the unemployment has been eliminated and people are back at work and it looks as if he is doing some good things in the construction." . . . As far as my mother—who also had the chance to leave with my sister and me—was concerned . . . she had a powerful position [in her job] and made good money. . . . She saw if we left and went to another country, we would have to struggle and start from scratch, and there were stories coming back about people who had to work as cleaning women and laundresses and servants and so forth and, to her, this was such horror that she simply could not face it.

To me, as a young girl, of course, this meant nothing. . . . To me the most overwhelming sense that I had was as if I were in a sort of glass enclosure in a giant prison, and I could see everybody . . . but nobody could see me and I could not get out. I was caught, and the only way I could keep my equilibrium mentally was to keep aware of what was happening. . . . It did not seem to me that the grownups or adults around me had that same impression or sense. It seemed that they kept adjusting each time that there was another limitation. . . . I suppose that also there was the feeling that, well, one day this was going to be over and it's a passing phase.

[Also] there were . . . several periods when, seemingly, the pressures were relaxing. One of those periods was in '36 during the Olympic Games. Just before that, after the Nuremberg Laws, the benches in the parks were painted yellow and marked for . . . non-Aryans only while the other benches were green. . . . About a week before the Olympic games started, these benches were suddenly painted green and, in general, you could see that if we wanted to go anywhere or use transportation or go to a movie . . . there would be no problem. . . . There were many foreigners on the streets and it became a marvelous experience. . . . I had the sense that I . . . would like to go up to someone in that street who looked like a foreigner and say, "Do you know what's happening to us Jews here? Do you care? Does anyone out there know about it?" . . . But I didn't dare to, of course. You had no way of knowing who the person was that you were speaking to. . . . Jesse Owens had these marvelous achievements of winning the gold medals and I recall going to the movies and seeing how . . . the Germans at the games had done everything to harass him and prevent him from winning. They made him start over again and they claimed that there was a wind at his back and whatever, and each time, he ran even faster than the time before. I was sitting there thoroughly relishing every moment of this experience, and around me the Germans in the audience were sitting there in complete silence. . . . Of course, I didn't make any comments. . . . A week after the Olympic Games were over, the benches were again painted yellow.

Each time there was this loosening-up experience, some Jews would say, "You see, something is going on. Things are getting a little bit better." And their will to deceive themselves that eventually things might, in fact, get better was so strong that it overcame their reservations about the reality of the situation.

After Susan finished high school, she went to a commercial school in a small Silesian town where she lived with some Orthodox family members and worked in their store.

Everybody there knew that you were Jewish [yet] I felt less hostility there than I did in Berlin. . . . It was impossible for us to participate in . . . any general cultural or social function. . . . The Jewish community was much more isolated in that city than it had been in Berlin and yet, in some ways, I felt more comfortable there. Perhaps because there was more of a sense of . . . being among your own kind, there was a certain sense of protection. . . . The young Jewish people there [were] trying to carry on life as usual. . . . I didn't feel that any of them had that same sense of precariousness.

On the train [back to Berlin] I got into a conversation with a man who was a postal clerk. . . . He said, "Oh, what a nice girl" I was and I seemed so bright. . . . I don't know how I got to talk about it, but he said he always knew what Jews were like. They smelled so terrible and they looked so awful. . . . He could always tell a Jew. And of course I said nothing and we just kept on talking. . . . When he was about to step off the train . . . I said to him, "Didn't you say that you could always tell a Jew when you met one?'' and he said, ''Oh yes, I certainly can,'' and I said, ''Well, you missed one.'' And he almost fell off the train, and that was one of the very few satisfactions that I had in those years. . . . I really felt a little bit vindicated.

For the next year Susan worked as a secretary in an emigration office, organizing the files of documents of those applying for emigration.

The Nazis had now decided that they would even encourage emigration . . . and it was specifically organized by the Germans to channel the Jewish money into the German coffers.

I was now exposed to daily pressures that were really beyond belief of the few emigration possibilities that were available as against the people that wanted to leave. . . . At this time it was late '37 and early '38 and things had become much more difficult. . . . Each day we would get notification of perhaps . . . six visas that were offered for the Dominican Republic to work . . . in the jungles, to clear the forest. . . . Practically all the jobs that were offered were invariably physical labor and required the kind of training that none of the Jews that were applying for emigration could possibly have had. And somehow we managed to evade and lie and change things. . . . A few people always managed to get out but it was a constant, terrible, terrible struggle. You . . . got the feeling that there was constant pressure, like a tremendous water pressure coming through a tight little water faucet so that only a few little trickles are coming out of the bottom and that was the trickle of people that were being let out to leave the country and allowed into foreign countries.

I remember one particular incident. . . . I was always one of the first to come in the morning . . . and I got there to find a man sitting there, very thin and pale and shaking like a leaf, and it turned out that he had just been released that morning . . . from a concentration camp and had been given twenty-four hours in which to leave the country. . . . Within the next eight or ten hours, we had to manage to get all of his papers together . . . to find a country that would take him . . . to get him on a boat and get him out of the country. . . . He couldn't talk and . . . I had to fill the form out for him because his hand was shaking so much. And I started to shake myself just to see him in this situation. . . . We managed to get him out.

As the tension increased, the family decided to register for emigration themselves. Fortunately for Susan and her mother and sister, they were able to get visas for Guatemala through the help of relatives living there. From there they would wait for their quota number to enter the United

States. But just before the details of their emigration were worked out, they experienced Crystal Night.[1]

It was a dark, sort of a greyish day, hazy and slightly warm for November and somehow there was some kind of electricity in the air that we sort of had a feeling to stay at home, be cautious. . . . Then after dark, my aunt with her husband came and they told us that there was already destruction going on outside. . . . And then my mother . . . sent me out into the streets of Berlin on the night of Crystal Night, the pogrom ongoing then, to buy, believe it or not, pork chops, because after all, the guests could not go without a proper dinner. I had to go to the northern part of Berlin to find a butcher shop that was still open [where they would not know me]. . . . I was walking over the sidewalks with glass crunching under my feet, and on the next street—Fasanenstrasse. . . . the oldest synagogue in Berlin . . . was in flames. The firetrucks were there training their hoses on the neighboring houses, but letting the synagogue burn. . . . And the entire sidewalk across from the synagogue was filled with hundreds of people . . . as if it was like a carnival to them . . . applauding and laughing . . . flames lighting up in the sky . . . and the people standing in the reflected light, in the glow of the flames . . . laughing. . . . I tried to walk past them in such a way that they wouldn't see that I was crying. . . . Then . . . there were some brown shirts and they were beating up an old Jewish man with a long beard . . . and there were people standing around laughing and applauding . . . like a Roman circus. . . . I came home and I was promptly sick all over the kitchen floor.

All I wanted was just get out, get out. I couldn't wait. And the last days were filled with all kinds of terrible situations because we had to sell . . . practically all of our belongings in order to raise what money we needed to pay for the tickets for the ship. . . . A man came to buy our furniture from us and, of course, realizing what our situation was, he gave us almost nothing for our furniture, and we had no choice but to accept his offer. My mother told me I could not take my books along. . . . Since I was a small child I had accumulated hundreds of books people had given me. . . . I could take only three books and it was something I never got over.

It was a traumatic time also because I would have to separate from my boyfriend. . . . We felt that relationships were tenuous. We did not know if we would ever see each other again and, somehow, whenever he and I were together, we always had the sense that this might be the last time, and every time together became a very emotionally charged situation. . . . [But] I sort of felt we would meet again and it would all be over.

[1]In German, *Kristallnacht*, literally night of broken glass. Refers to pogroms in Germany and Austria on November 9–10, 1938, in which many synagogues and much Jewish property was destroyed. Some Jews were injured and killed and thirty-five thousand Jewish men were sent to concentration camps.

They left on November 18, 1938, one week after Crystal Night.

After we left Hamburg, the ship docked at Antwerp where we met our father. He had left Germany in early May of '38 after he had been warned that he would be picked up that night. He was leading a precarious existence as a refugee without papers. We did not realize at that time that this day would be the last we would spend together. After many vicissitudes, he was killed in Auschwitz in late 1942.

Susan, her mother, and her sister were able to get to Guatemala after a prolonged journey around the tip of South America to avoid the naval blockades. After two years there, they were finally able to enter the United States. Susan was nineteen-years-old.

As I look back, it seemed to me that those Jews in Germany who had a closer Jewish identity . . . had a slightly better time of it because they did have a sense of their identity and there was a certain feeling of mutual protectiveness, however ephemeral it might have been. . . . I had nothing positive in a Jewish image to hold against the caricatures and the vilification that I was hearing daily. . . . There was somehow to my immature mind . . . enough in all of this talk to make me feel that possibly there might be something in it. . . . I had no mature judgment to set against it and I had nothing but . . . fear around me and . . . a world of adults . . . who really didn't want to discuss the entire situation.

For the first several years after, all I wanted to do was just forget about it all. . . . I realized many years later that I had gone the wrong road and that I could no longer live that life of . . . denial of my Jewish identity. . . . I then, finally . . . went back and tried to recover my Jewish identity or, rather, build one which I never had . . . to gain some kind of equilibrium. But it has never been easy.

I hope . . . to continue what little I can do to maintain the memories and to be a witness to those events . . . what made the German Jews act as they did during those years . . . the reality of what it was like to live under this kind of a dictatorship. . . . Those of us that had some knowledge of what went on in those early years of the Nazi period must retain consciousness of it and must speak out. . . . We must be alert to the early warning signs.

From the testimony of Susan Neulaender Faulkner

2   *Anne Dore*

Anne Dore was the daughter of an anti-Nazi Social Democratic family in Germany. During the war, her father maintained his political and moral integrity despite social ostracism and loss of his civil service job because he refused to become a Nazi Party member. He supported Anne Dore in her struggle to uphold a similar strength of character, an unpopular and dangerous position in a climate of hatred and fear.

The Social Democratic Party, which had been outlawed by Bismarck, struggled to bring about a parliamentary democracy and social reform. By November 1918, the Kaiser had to abdicate and the Social Democrats found themselves in charge of a new government—a republic. However, Germans suffered from the humiliating defeat of World War I, unemployment, inflation, and political instability. The Social Democrats were blamed for all of these problems and were particularly scapegoated by the rising Nazi Party. They and the Jews were also blamed for the German defeat—the ''stab in the back.'' All political parties except the Nazis were eliminated by Hitler's takeover in 1933, but the fury toward the Social Democrats and Jews for causing Germany's problems persisted.

Anne Dore's childhood years in Germany paralleled the Nazi period. Born in 1926, she started school in 1933 and graduated in 1945. Her family lived in Brandenburg, thirty miles west of Berlin, in a semi-rural, middle- to lower-middle-class community. Her father was a civil servant in municipal administration in the area and belonged to the Social Democratic Party (SPD). With the Nazi takeover in 1933 he immediately lost his job because he was not a member of the Nazi party. He applied repeatedly for compensation for his lost job, and after two years finally received the minimum allowed. In the meantime, he retrained as an accountant so that he could work in private industry apart from the Nazi-controlled civil service.

But his struggle to maintain his political and moral integrity continued, and he carefully instructed Anne Dore from her earliest years.

In our neighborhood, for instance, there were people that belonged to the Nazi party and they just slid along, so to speak, to keep their jobs. But we also had the neighborhood officials that reported directly to the party and they were the dedicated people. You were taught from early on in Germany that the way to greet people was to use the "*Heil* Hitler" salute and if you refused to do that as an adult, you would occasionally run a risk of being turned in, and my father told us not to use that. We could use it in school—that was beyond his control— but, privately, when we went for walks and met people, we would always say "*Guttentag*" and never "*Heil* Hitler." As the Nazi time progressed and we entered the war, that became actually an act of opposition and it was quite [risky].

During her early school years, Anne Dore had to sort out the contradictory messages she was getting—from her teachers and her father.

For the first three years of my grade school training [in] a one room rural school . . . I remember having an old teacher . . . who was a member of the Nazi party. I remember seeing his lapel and that little bon-bon [Nazi insignia] on there. However, he was an interesting man and I liked my school experience a whole lot because I was put together with kids of all ages. He didn't talk a whole lot about the Nazi [theory] but he was a real bug on physical fitness. . . . You had to be fit to serve your Führer.

He [also] integrated political propaganda in various fields of instruction. One example that I remember vividly was that . . . I was a very good little artist and I liked to draw. In the pre-Christmas time, I drew a Santa Claus and he had his knapsack full of gifts for children and he had a flag sticking which was a swastika flag. And I was lauded for a good rendition of this flag and I was very proud that it was shown to all the other age kids and held up as a model of good art. When I took it home to my father, he took me aside and said, "Don't ever do this sort of thing again. We are ashamed of this flag. This man Hitler has even changed the flag in Germany and we don't want to show it and you shouldn't show it in connection with Santa Claus."

After these first three years, Anne Dore was placed in the city school system and the stigma of her father's political views became increasingly evident.

What followed me there was that everytime I was put in [a class] my dad's name was recognized. . . . They said, "Was he the Social Democrat?" and I would say, "Yes," so that there was always a slight suspicion on the part of a lot of these administrators of who I would be like.

I always felt put on a carpet because I had to prove that I was a good student, that I was as good or better than the others, because politically my family was suspect. I never felt, really, that I was being persecuted for that [but] I was on my toes half the time.

I would come home and discuss certain things with my father, and he would always set me right on things . . . [so] I was checked and balanced very well. . . . In a political system of that time, you learned very early that you couldn't say everything that you thought, that you thought twice before you said certain things to certain people, and that you also felt you were justified in lying—that is, paying a certain amount of lip service in order to appear non-suspect. When you switched from the school to the home, you operated on two different planes. My fortune was that I had a father who constantly supervised and guided me and balanced me in my views.

In such a small town, the families of Anne Dore's classmates were aware of her father's background.

The political background of your parents was usually quite apparent because you knew what profession they belonged to, what positions they held, and in Germany traditionally—or it used to be traditionally—[there was] a tremendous degree of class consciousness. . . . You knew where you fit in. . . . The others knew that my dad was a fired civil servant, so that this also meant that he couldn't be trusted on the Nazistic base.

In turn, Anne Dore's friendships were affected.

When you had an intimate relationship with a close friend, you would occasionally talk about things of political nature. The easy way was always to leave it out and limit yourself to school and recreational activities. . . . I was withdrawn because actually I was taught to be on my toes and I don't think that helped being very sociable. . . . I did not have too many friends. I had some very good girlfriends, but just a few, maybe two.

When I started high school—that was in 1936–37—the situation had already gotten critical . . . and some Jewish families had already moved from my area.

I remember that there were one or two girls in school who were what was called then half-Jewish—whatever that was—and they were accepted, but they stood out. Everybody was aware of them and so you had the attitude of the Nazi daughters to ignore them and the others falling over backwards to be extra special nice, so that they really had a hard time being like everybody else. And, all of a sudden, in 1938, they disappeared. That coincided somehow with the *Kristallnacht* activities that they were forced to be taken out of the public schools.

Besides the photographs of the destruction and vandalism in the local papers, Anne Dore's recollections of *Kristallnacht* focus primarily on her father's explanation and his reaction.

My father . . . told me that the Nazis went in and that they invited the population to loot. [Afterwards he explained] to me that from then on the Nazis would keep a record of anyone insisting on shopping in these stores. And a week later, I remember that my dad had to go to get a pair of shoes and went to a store that had been boarded up but was opened again, and the local paper published his name and showed him in front of the store, saying that he insists on buying from Jews.

We really didn't know whether the [Jewish] families had a chance to emigrate . . . or whether they were deported. . . . My father knew that they were leaving, and I don't know under what circumstances. . . . However, I knew about some families that owned department stores that my grandfather had business relations with. They stayed in town waiting for a visa to leave for Australia and during that time, they were under a state of house arrest. . . . It had been indicated to them that it wouldn't be safe for them to be seen in the streets any more and they had young children and asked my grandfather would it be possible that the nanny could take the kids into our garden so that they could get fresh air and use the swing. And I remember that they came twice a week and very cautiously just walked through the garden to play in the sandbox and use the swing. And I looked at them. I couldn't understand why they didn't go to the public park, and my grandfather . . . took me aside and said, "I don't want you to talk about it. It's none of your business. These kids will use the swing and you will share it with them, and you will understand later on why we do this." And so, I had a feeling that they were very special people. However, in what way they were special, I did not fully understand.

I think they made it out before the war broke out and emigrated to Australia. That's the last I heard.

I also remember that my pediatrician, when I was a little kid, was a man by the name of Dr. Lansberger whom I really loved. He was a very gentle man, and we applied for another check-up and I was looking forward to going there, and all of a sudden—that was in 1937—we went there and he was gone. And then my dad said he left because it wasn't safe for the family, and I think they emigrated to the United States.

My grandparents lived in a worker's district in an apartment building. They owned it and . . . next door . . . there was a Jewish worker who lived there with his three children. They were put on a terrible ration system, much lower than anyone else. . . . And my grandmother would always make sure that, since she had an orchard, this woman could come over and get fruit for her kids, and vegetables. . . . If they didn't show up for a week, she would send us over and say, "Tell her there is food here." . . . They did survive.

Persecution took many [forms]. I remember that we had an elderly couple next door, in that same house, and they were Jehovah's Witnesses and the husband was taken and he did not survive. . . . If he promised to sign that he would never follow his faith, they said they would let him go, and he didn't, and I think he was beaten to death. I remember that.

Anne Dore's uncle was also caught in the Nazi web because of his political stance.

My uncle . . . was a city manager in Brandenburg and exposed in the sense that he also . . . was a speaker in the State Parliament belonging to the SPD . . . and as soon as the Nazis came to power . . . they rolled up at three o'clock in the morning with the truck in front of the house . . . hammered on the gate . . . pushed past [my aunt] and pulled him out of bed in his pajamas and threw him on the truck and he disappeared. . . . He returned [from] Sachsenhausen . . . after about two months. . . . He had been a very rotund, very healthy looking man and when he came back he had lost a hundred pounds. He refused to talk about any of his experiences to the family and he couldn't look anyone in the eye. He always looked down. He was in a prolonged state of depression and shock and it took him about a year to work his way to some degree of normalcy. And when Hitler's headquarters in East Prussia were blown up by a rebellion of his officers in 1944, he was rounded up again alongside a lot of the people that belonged to the underground . . . and he was . . . sent back to Sachsenhausen . . . for about two months. . . . He was sent out with the warning that if he took up any contacts with any member of the underground, he would be hanged. So, overtly, he stayed very neutral, stayed in the house, didn't move around, didn't make any phone calls and survived until the end of the war. . . . He did recover and he was again very active in reconstructing the Social Democratic Party.

Another man, close to Anne Dore and her family, was scarred more permanently.

He was, in the beginning of the Nazi era, quite sympathetic to the system. He had risen [in the ranks] and felt very important and tried to indicate to my father that he wasn't following the right course in his resistance to accept that system. . . . This man was drafted into the infantry . . . and sent to the Eastern Front. . . . A year later or so his wife suddenly received news from a sanitorium, a rehabilitation hospital, and we were a little bit surprised. . . . When he came back he visited my father and he was in uniform . . . and we didn't even recognize him. . . . He looked very worn and he was white-haired and he was very nervous and he had lost a lot of weight. And my father asked him in and he said, "I would like to talk to you, but I can't do it here. Can we go out and go for a walk in your garden?" . . . He actually cried. He apologized to [my father] and he said, "You were so right about that system."

They had sent him to Russia and at first he was just part of the occupying force and one of the days [they] rounded up his whole platoon for special duty. And they took him to a village and he found out . . . that they had been detached to be an execution platoon. They were taken out into the open area some place quite a way from the rest of the troops and were told that they would have to shoot these civilian people. He recognized that they had been Jewish people that were driven out of the villages and rounded up. . . . And as they were getting ready [and] they got the orders to shoot, this man just fainted and went beserk . . . and had to be taken to the mental institution. . . . He was an eyewitness and I think he, as long as he lived, never forgot this. He mentioned it many times even after the war to my father . . . that he owed him an apology. He owed it to all kinds of people. But my father had predicted it and he didn't want to believe, and it had to go so far that he would be thrown into this situation before he could see. I don't think he ever completely recovered. He was depressed much of the time. . . . He had been a very active man, a stone mason, and I don't think he ever worked regularly after that.

Censorship of the press and incessant Nazi propaganda left BBC radio as the primary source of news for those Germans who would risk listening.

My father got up every night at 2:00 A.M. . . . when one of the broadcasts came on. . . . He would wait until everybody was in bed. We had a maid that lived in the house and we didn't know whether she was to be trusted, so we couldn't listen at 10 or 8. [So] he listened at 2:00 A.M. and he would take a wool blanket and put it over his head and then tune in the radio so that any kind of jamming distortion wouldn't be too much noise. . . . We would sit at breakfast in the morning and he would tell us the latest news about the various fronts and so on, and that, too, was quite dangerous. If you were caught or if somebody denounced you . . . you would end up in a camp someplace.

My grandmother had a blind cousin . . . quite advanced in years. . . . He listened [to the BBC] and had renters in his own little home and he had some kind of an argument with them, and, in revenge, they turned him in and he ended up in the penitentiary . . . and he was done away with by the Nazis. . . . He had to serve five years for listening to a foreign radio station, but he never survived . . . because he was "inferior" because of his blindness in addition to having listened to this foreign radio.

[My father] was well-informed because he listened to the BBC and he considered that a very objective newscast. My youngest brother started listening to Radio Moscow and my father was quite disturbed about that because he didn't trust the Russian news reports. . . . As the war progressed and things got worse and worse, there were more and more people that really did tune in on those broadcasts, and there was a kind of grapevine of people that knew each other that could compare notes. However, you had to be very careful and cautious whom you approached on these things.

About six weeks before the war ended, Anne Dore was taken out of her high school and put to work in a factory, the last surge of the German war effort.

Fighter planes were flying over and we were being bombed in our home town and the moods of the active Nazi population changed. You saw fewer and fewer brown uniforms. They were carefully folded up and not flaunted anymore, and you would see in the local paper, "We will fight with our last blood, our last drop of blood." As the Russians approached from the East by the end of April and we also heard that the Western Front had totally collapsed, we were told that our home town would be declared an open city, that there wouldn't be any unnecessary fighting and that our mayor, who was a Nazi-appointed active supporter of the system, would stick it out with us and help us through the difficult times. Within a week prior to the final occupation, this man took a Red Cross ambulance and left with his family . . . and gave himself up to the British troops. That was the kind of support that they provided.

The majority of the Nazi leadership really did flee. But some of my [Nazi] teachers in high school did not, and what we heard immediately after the occupation was that they were arrested . . . by the Russians . . . and disappeared towards the East. . . . But the local leadership had prudently removed themselves towards the West because they expected better treatment from the Americans and British and French troops.

After the war, Anne Dore's father was reinstated in the civil service and became the director of social work in Brandenburg.

The mayor then was a Communist and my dad was a Socialist, a life-long Socialist, [so that job] lasted for about two months and then they made him resign again because they didn't trust him. They thought he was not truly a fellow traveler of the system. . . . He was a very loyal local patriot and couldn't see to leave for the West and so . . . he went back in private industry.

Anne Dore began her university studies at the Humboldt University in East Berlin but Soviet control of the curriculum made her school experience oppressive. She transferred to the newly established Free University in West Berlin.

We were sort of charter members [of the Free University] helping it from the initial stage into being a more successful institution. . . . We were very active politically and needed a warm place to go . . . and that's where I had my initial contact with Hanna Silver [a young Jewish woman] who opened a home to a lot of hungry students . . . a warm place . . . a wonderful meal . . . and we were sitting in her home discussing politics after 1945.

Now they could look back to a time when political protest was forbidden and evaluate those who stood up to the Nazi domination from a different perspective.

Those people that actually harbored or helped Jews hide away obviously did never talk about it. . . . There was danger in ever mentioning things while it was going on, so they were very tight-lipped and very calm. As a matter of fact, they might have camouflaged it by being pro-Nazi so no one suspected anything. I knew about [such] a woman who helped by traveling to Switzerland and clearing passport possibilities and while going across the border [also] smuggling out assets for the family trying to leave.

I got very cynical . . . after the war because suddenly you heard of many people bragging or protesting that they had helped Jews. . . . I discarded a lot of these things as just trying to whitewash their . . . feelings of guilt. . . . I am sure that some people did [help]. But they were very often the ones that never talked about that.

From the testimony of Anne Dore Weidemann Russell

3   *David*

David was the child of a Jewish–Protestant marriage (with a Jewish father and Protestant mother) and therefore fell into the controversial muddle among Nazi officials seeking a Judenfrei (Jew-free) Germany. Because of this confusion, he was able to stay in his native Berlin throughout the war, escaping deportation yet constantly fearful of the time when his ambiguous status would collapse, when he and his father would be deported with the rest of the Jewish side of the family to the death camps. Joining other teenage boys who were also children of mixed marriages, he channeled his fury and feelings of vulnerability into small acts of sabotage as a member of one of the anonymous groups secretly webbed throughout the Reich.

Approximately 125,000 people of mixed religious background and 28,000 in mixed marriages within Germany and Austria in 1938 (called the Reich-Protectorate) remained largely immune from anti-Jewish measures. The survival rate for these groups within Germany itself remained especially high since no way was found to successfully disentangle them from the Aryan parts of their families. Until the end of the war, however, their fate remained uncertain; their lives hinged on their classification, continually threatened by the flick of a pen.

Today, David proudly displays several magnificent oil paintings of his German Jewish ancestors dating back to the mid-eighteenth century. His family played an important role in the economic development of Berlin and, as loyal patriots, his grandfather fought in the Prussian army in the

War of 1870 and his father was decorated with the Iron Cross in World War I.

David's father prospered as a partner in a private bank, in addition to having manufacturing and real estate interests. The family owned two five-story buildings on either side of their street, and their third-floor apartment was opposite that of a general retired from the Kaiser's army. On New Year's, the custom was to go out on the balcony and toast the neighbors with champagne. The old general, still flying the Imperial flag and refusing to replace it with the Nazi insignia, toasted them in return. David's friends were both Jewish and non-Jewish. After the war he discovered that the older brother of one of his friends had taken part in the attempt on July 20, 1944, to assassinate Hitler.

David was born in 1928 and his earliest memories of the Hitler period were seen through the eyes of a five-year-old. Storm troopers (SA) flanked the door of the corner bar near his home, designated as a polling place for the 1933 election—"intimidating . . . in full uniform, with a leather belt, brown shirt, and a swastika. . . . I still have the image." Since Jews were forbidden now to hold a mortgage, his father's real estate and business holdings were either confiscated or sold to Nazi sympathizers for far below market value. What was of most concern to young David was that his family could stay in their apartment for the time being, though they now paid rent to the new owner.

In elementary school, David faced increasing trouble.

Preferably, we were not seen on the street. . . . [We] got beaten up. . . . Suddenly kids started calling you "Jew." We spent very much time inside with . . . other Jewish friends . . . in '34 and '35 when it really started. . . . I had a little friend who lived across the street. We went to school together. You covered each other's back. You watched out for flying stones. . . . Some teachers already had anti-Semitic signs in the classroom. There was a particular teacher that . . . came over and explained to me that the sign didn't pertain to me. . . . It was . . . less harrassment, as I recall, and more separation.

The sign "didn't pertain" to David because he was not a full Jew by Nazi definition—his father was Jewish and his mother Protestant—even though he was being raised as a Jew. His status protected him, but created painful problems.

We lost not only friends, but we lost family on my mother's side—with the exception of one aunt—who suddenly didn't know us any more . . . until after World War II when they suddenly appeared on the scene again. . . . Until 1936 we used to visit once a year. We used to stay a week or so. Then they stopped writing. . . . I think it grieved [my mother] no end. . . . They didn't want contact. They were afraid for themselves. I think that's what it was, because fear had set in by that time. . . . Neighbor looked at neighbor . . . looking over their shoulder. . . .

My parents weren't very scientific . . . [and] as odd as it may seem . . . if they had friends over during those years and if they sat talking in the living room . . . they would take a big pillow and put it over the telephone. . . . Apparently somebody had told them that the Nazis already were able to listen in over the telephone even though it was hung up. Of course, it is impossible, but . . . that is just an indication of the fear that already existed at that time.

Although David's parents were aware of the impending danger before 1935, his father did not apply to emigrate until 1937 or 1938.

You know, I used to blame the older generation. . . . I've always blamed them for that. You see, they were Germans, don't forget. They weren't Jews. Judaism was a religion, just like here. You're an American; you're not a Jew. Okay? I mean they always had been Germans, and their fathers had been German. Didn't he serve in World War I? Didn't he fight for the Fatherland? So who's this corporal . . . ? It will go away. That was the attitude. It will go away. But by '35 we began to wonder what would happen. We began to worry about things in '36 and '37. And in '38 came the Crystal Night and my father's friend, who had lost an arm and a leg in World War I, was pulled out on the street . . . and brutally beaten.

For ten-year-old David, Crystal Night of November 1938 was terrifying.

We lived on the third floor, but you heard the glass shattering, you heard the screaming, the hollering, the banging on doors. . . . Shattering of glass— I will never forget that. I remember that I crawled under the couch that day. . . . [But] I think they didn't want to climb that high. Three floors up. I was safe. It was mostly the first floor and the stores.

As the situation worsened, David's family was forced to move. They were given one week to close up their large apartment and move into one room in another smaller apartment which they shared with two other families.

Then life in one room started. It was remarkable—you had a bed and you had to put a curtain across. You had your own rooms within a room.

   Although they had to sell many of their possessions, they were able
to store some with German friends and many of their precious family
photographs, documents, and paintings with his aunt, his mother's sister,
who also lived in Berlin throughout the war.

   [By this time] ration cards had started . . . and Jews were not permitted to have
meat or milk, eggs, less bread, less vegetables, no fish, no sugar. . . . You just
didn't get rations from that. So we really lived on my mother's rations. She got
full rations. Thanks to her, it helped.

   After the Jewish children were banned from the public schools, David
attended an academic Jewish high school, the Holdheim School, one of
two such institutions in Berlin. After a time, the two schools were combined and put into makeshift quarters in a synagogue.

   The education was good for one reason . . . that somehow we had to prove
that we were just as good if not better than everybody else. There was an intensive
training. And then, you couldn't do anything else anyway by that time.

   To protect the children from danger in the streets after class hours, the
school provided activities, from ping pong to Jewish cultural programs.
But by 1940, David's school of about three hundred children was being
depleted.

   And, then, kids would disappear from school. First, we would know they had
to leave. . . . It was like moving somewhere, like they moved to Warsaw. In
fact, I got postcards from school friends of mine in Warsaw. Of course, they
couldn't say much, that they were fine and blah, blah, blah. . . . They could pack
all of their belongings, all this make-believe, and they shipped them out with
big crates. . . . At that time, it wasn't looked at as too serious. Not then. . . . [But
soon] rather rapidly they were being picked up. . . . They just closed the schools
down. . . . By the way, out of the three hundred kids . . . and you get to know
each other . . . it was very cramped . . . and you get to know most kids . . . only
three out of three hundred that I know of came out of it.

   During these deportations, David became a Bar Mitzvah in Berlin.

   I was good friends with the rabbi's son. So his father trained me. . . . The big
synagogues had been burned [during Crystal Night]. This was where the school
was . . . in the back of the building. . . . It had escaped damage because . . . it
wasn't apparent from the street. . . . That was probably the only reason that it

did escape. It was a small synagogue . . . [but] I was just as scared of going up there and . . . reading from the Torah as I was of everything else.

The meaning of David's mixed status was driven home again and again. For about nine or ten months after the schools closed,

I worked in the . . . *Reichsvereinigung der Juden in Deutschland*[1] . . . the central organization of the Jews in Germany. . . . I was an office helper . . . so that I would have something to do. . . . until the day they picked the people up, when the SS came and Gestapo came . . . and the trucks were down there and they lined everybody up, and they pushed me forward. Somebody who knew me said, "His mother's Protestant," and they said, "Okay, you can leave." I went past the guards, I went home, half in shock, because they had already taken the people down into the trucks, you know, furniture vans, closed the doors and off they went. That was the last I saw of them. . . . They didn't come back. . . . I never saw anyone again who was there. We have the list up to '45, a long list of names. . . . An office had opened. The people could find out if their friends had come back. Nobody came back.

David and his family searched the war news for clues to their unpredictable fate.

The hope started after Stalingrad [winter of 1942–1943]. We knew that was the turning point. Everybody knew. That's when the hope started. That's when I put maps up and the little flags and I started measuring distances. Because, you know, suddenly your lifeline depended on little flags and the distance between them. That was, you had to hold on until that time.

In the meantime their daily existence remained uncertain and the Gestapo threat more terrifying.

By that time they weren't polite anymore. There was no week [for] packing. . . . If they got you on the street, they just grabbed you.

On February 27, 1943, it was David and his father who were grabbed.

We ended up at the *Rosenstrasse* [Camp in Berlin]. . . . They separated those that had Aryan wives . . . and we sat on the fourth floor of the building. . . . It was also the first bombing of Berlin at the same time. . . . It scared me, you

---

[1]Federal Union of Jews in Germany, to which all Jews, under the Nazi definition, were compelled to belong. It was created by the Nazis in July 1939. An earlier organization, created by the Jews in 1933, was voluntary.

know. Scared like anything. All kinds of people just sitting on the floor. . . .
There was no furniture at all, people just laid on top of each other up there. And
there was a demonstration. I think it was the only demonstration against Hitler
during that era. The women of those people inside were demonstrating outside
. . . screaming, "We want our husbands back." . . . The police were trying to
hold them back. Nobody knew what happened [but] due to connections—many
of these people in Berlin were related in some fashion to important people . . .
I think that's what saved them. We were released after a week. . . . For instance,
I had a friend; his mother was related to . . . a World War I hero . . . a German
Air Force general, a very important man at the time. Hitler had him killed [later]
in '43, I think, but then he was a very important man. . . . People had connections.
It was a big city.

[But during that week I was] scared, real scared. Just plain, plain scared. . . .
I didn't think. I didn't know what to think. I didn't know what was happening
to me at that time. . . . [I remember] we were taken down to the yard and walked
in a circle for maybe half an hour and went upstairs again and sat around. And
some food was issued. Soup. Minimal.

[When the protest started] everybody ran. . . . Everybody piled against the
windows. . . . I couldn't see over everybody. Everybody was looking for everybody. My mother was outside. . . . Yes, yes. She was out there, too.

I remember the fellow. In fact, I still have the piece of paper, ostensibly
yellow, the release sheet, the yellow star, *Der Jude*, The Jew, Released. I
remember that he addressed us before we were released, and he cut a very
dashing figure in his black SS uniform, and he was icily polite saying, "Gentlemen, I'm sorry I can't send you to the concentration camp." I will never forget
that. "I can't send you to the concentration camp."

After the *Rosenstrasse Aktion*, David and his father, along with the
others, were required to report to a local police station and were soon
assigned to a labor unit, his father doing carpentry and repairing bomb
damage and David to a work gang restoring steel helmets and mess kits,
sixty hours a week with no pay.

You worked and you got rations and if you didn't produce then you go to the
concentration camp. . . . You sort of lived in the foyer of these camps, so to
speak. . . . We feared for the worst. . . .

I don't know. . . . I was mad. I was scared and I was mad and I used to blame
the older generation all through that period, until even after the war. I used to
tell my father, "It's your fault. You let it happen." His generation, not he
personally. I said that you should have fought. In fact, we did fight. Not he. I
did. . . . Well, you fight back in Germany or leave. One or the other. Don't take
it. . . . I joined the resistance group in Berlin in 1943. A group of fellows that I

worked with, one of the school friends that was still around, also from a mixed marriage. . . .

We met privately. . . . One of them had contacts with some other group and never disclosed who he was in contact with. Especially in the last years of the war, especially during the Battle of Berlin, we, I think, did our share to fight back. . . . We cut telephone wires and interrupted communications, cut tires on army cars that were parked on side streets.

The group was made up of six young men between fourteen and eighteen years old, mostly from mixed marriages. They were active from 1943 until the war ended and none of them was ever caught.

The spirit was excellent, in . . . that we had very few weapons. I think out of the six, we had two revolvers and I think about twenty rounds of ammunition, something like that. The idea was that they are not going to get us. That was the attitude.

[We] filled the mess kit [to be repaired] with acid, and the acid was so strong if you left a piece of aluminum in there overnight, the next morning it wouldn't be there anymore. It would be completely dissolved. . . . So we would fill a mess kit full of acid and put it in a sack of finished goods, and it was shipped out to the German army and you can imagine how much was left when it got there. Some of the, maybe, juvenile things that we thought up.

One fellow got the information . . . what they wanted us to do. . . . There was some kind of organization—limited—I don't think very effective, to be honest. I don't think that what we did made a hound's tooth of difference, but it made a big difference to me. I am a great believer in "Never again." No next time around. No. . . . [My parents] tried to talk me out of it [because of the danger]. . . . I think that is why I left Germany [after the war].

David's experience with the German people themselves varied markedly. On the one hand, he describes his father wearing the yellow star being beaten up on the street for being a "—— Jew"; another time his father was approached by two German workers who pointed to the star in disbelief, exclaiming, "Man, what the —— are you wearing? What's that? You got to wear that? . . . Oh, these b——!"

The Berliners were not necessarily Nazis per se. Berlin was a very cosmopolitan town. . . . I had a similar happening to me. I walked down the street coming home and suddenly a man approached me with a bag in his hand and he said, "Come into the doorway," and before you know it he said, "Take this," and he threw the bag in my hand and took off. I looked and there were two loaves of bread in it, some butter, and some food. . . . It has always been somehow reminiscent of God asking [Abraham] if you find ten just men I will not destroy Sodom and Gomorrah. So there were some just people around. It has been my experience.

During the final bombardment of Berlin, David's neighbors sought shelter in what he describes as a "Jewish cellar" and an "Aryan cellar." When a stray shell implanted itself in the Jewish cellar,

I must say to the credit of the other . . . oh, we had some Nazis in the building that wouldn't look at you [but] the Nazis had left by then—but [it was] to the credit of the rest of the people that [in] the last couple days . . . before the Russians took the city we were invited in the Aryan cellar.

David's status as the child of a mixed marriage had protected him so far, but the family never knew when the Nazi guidelines might change.

[Until the very end of the war] we feared for the worst. In fact, the worst would have come in May of '45. The order had already been given in Berlin that mixed marriages . . . would be separated [as had already been done in other German towns] . . . and then [my father and I would be] shipped to the camps. Lucky for us, the Russians got in the way of the plans and then the Battle of Berlin started.

By that time I was used to air attacks. . . . It is kind of interesting to sit there and hope that your friends [flying the planes] will miss you. And it's also interesting to note that I had a cousin in the German Air Force and I had a cousin in the British intelligence. You know . . . this kind of family situation.

As early as 1943, David's family had news of the death camps, the ghettos, and the massacres on the Eastern Front from soldiers passing through Berlin.

That cousin in the German Air Force came back from Russia in 1945. . . . He told us he was stationed in Latvia and that their airfield was near a gas works and it had been burned out and that [they] brought the people and lined them up and shot them with machine guns. Their commander said, "We are the Air Force and we don't have anything to do with it, so don't look." So people knew, I don't care what anybody says. If somebody says that they didn't know, I don't believe it.

At the end of the war, David's family

suddenly discovered they had relatives in Berlin again. . . . Suddenly my parents were invited to come and visit, and life went back to normalcy. . . . [As for my aunt] she lived in Berlin and that contact was never lost . . . and there were people in the building who were anti-Nazi. As I said, we had experiences that gave you hope.

But if it had not been for the protection and rations brought by his mother's non-Jewish status, fate for David and his father might have been very different.

No question about it. . . . All my relatives on my father's side never came back. . . .

[After the war] amazingly, everybody was looking to the future . . . but I frankly left Germany in 1948 because I couldn't look anybody in the face, because in my mind was a question: Where were you? . . . I almost threw someone out of the subway in 1945 after the war who made anti-Semitic remarks. . . . And all the "good Germans" stood around silently and didn't say a word, just as they stood around when the Nazis beat up the Jews. . . . I wouldn't take it lying down.

From the testimony of David . . .

4   *Hans*

---

*Hans is a German Gypsy who gave an eyewitness account of Josef Men-
gele's medical experimentation in Auschwitz at a public hearing at the 1985
Gathering of Holocaust Survivors in Philadelphia. He shared this testimony, spoken in his native German, with our interviewer, supplementing
his concentration camp experience with his earlier life story. He recounted
the warm, tradition-bound family life of the pre-war European Gypsy, the
colorful trek of their carnival during his childhood summers, then the Nazi
persecution of Gypsies, and his frenzied efforts to escape. Although in mortal
danger, his acting background enabled him to use life-saving disguises, while
his extended family was sought out for protection.*

*The destruction of the Gypsy population of Europe paralleled in many
ways that of the Jews, though at a more uneven pace and with some
exceptions. Since Hungary and Romania were German allies, Gypsies in
those countries were not harmed. Moreover, Himmler believed that Gypsies
of Sinti and Lalleri stock may have been descended from the same Indo-
Germanic group as Aryans. Nazi scientists attempted to classify Gypsies
according to racial blood types, just as they did with the Jews. They also
labeled the Gypsy population as a criminal element, born thieves, agita-
tors, and arsonists, a danger to public order.*

*From the time of the first deportations in 1939, Gypsies were sent along
with Jews to the Polish ghettos and later concentration camps from all
German-controlled lands. The thirty to forty thousand Gypsies within the
Reich, over a million in all of Europe, were deemed parasites and the
''Gypsy question,'' as the ''Jewish question,'' was to be answered by the
Final Solution. Although we do not yet have accurate figures, it is estimated*

that one-fourth to one-third of the Gypsies in Europe were murdered—
possibly a half-million. They were killed in the massacres of the Einsatz-
gruppen (mobile killing units accompanying the German troops into Soviet
territory), mass shootings in Serbia and Croatia, gassings throughout the
killing centers, and medical experimentation such as that in Auschwitz.

Hans is a German Gypsy whose roots stretch back through the generations to India. Born in Hanover, Germany, in 1923, Hans, his parents,
and ten younger siblings traveled by horse-drawn wagon throughout the
countryside during the summer months, carrying a small carnival with
swings, merry-go-round, shooting gallery, and music. In the winter, they
would stay at their "home place" in Bernau near Berlin. Anti-Gypsy
sentiment was not a problem during Hans' early childhood and they
continued to travel through Germany unmolested even after Hitler came
to power in 1933. According to Hans,

the persecution of the Gypsies started after the Jews, our co-sufferers. . . . In
1939, when the war started, then the persecution started also. . . . Our rations
were like those of the Jews, limited to half [the Aryan allotment of] sugar, flour,
etc. [We had] little meat, as was usual. We also were not permitted to leave
our home compound [where] we lived together in our "living wagon." . . . We
had to sign papers that we would not leave home. . . . Otherwise we were to be
punished. . . . Like the Jews had to wear the Star of David, we had to wear the
"Z."[1]
   In 1940 to 1941, it started to get extreme. We were not permitted to leave
our compound and we had to abide by it. We were drafted for work in the
armament industry for the German army. . . . Father had to work in a munitions
factory. I had to work in a cartridge factory. . . . We were paid but not like skilled
labor, not enough to pay for our rations. Father had on the side a little transport
business. We had a few horses which later were taken away from us.
   A great change came in 1941. One day I was called for night shift . . . and
during this night shift my machine broke. I must have unfortunately put one part
into the machine the wrong way. . . . They sent me home. . . . In the morning
about 9:00 A.M. came two gentlemen from the Gestapo and wanted to arrest me.
. . . My mother saw them coming. I got dressed in a hurry, went through a
window, over the fence, and ran away.

Hans fled to the next railway station and took the train to Berlin where
he hid with his grandfather and uncle.

[1]For *Zigeuner*, the German word for Gypsy.

A few days [later] the Gestapo appeared again at my grandfather's. They knew where our families lived. . . . Fortunately my uncle had sent me . . . to buy him some cigarettes and [while] they searched for me . . . my uncle said to his son, who was about eight years old, to warn me not to come back.

Now that his grandfather's house was too dangerous a hiding place, sixteen-year-old Hans found another location down the street through the help of some friends.

[But this house] was kind of taboo for us [because] the man was a pallbearer by profession. . . . I always had to return to my grandfather to eat. . . . The danger was great and constant.

His next move was to an uncle in the Sudetenland, but it ended a month later with another visit from the Gestapo: "I suppose today that they wanted to accuse me of sabotage." Following the Gypsy network, Hans escaped to Luxembourg where he was provided with false papers and stayed safely for a year.

[During this time] I longed so much for my parents and sisters and brothers . . . that I dared to take the train to Berlin. Mother picked me up and took me secretly to Bernau. I was there only two days when the Gestapo turned up again. Again I ran away.

Hans sought out an uncle in Bamberg whose sons were in the German army, hoping that this would provide him with increased protection.

Somehow I felt free there and went for a walk in town . . . with my cousin. . . . I did not wear [the "Z" patch] anymore. My cousin wore the German army uniform. I was pretty sure that not much could happen to me. . . . Suddenly a police car stopped. . . . They arrested both of us and incarcerated us in Bamberg. I was there in jail for four weeks. My cousin's uniform was taken off, he was discharged, and also put in jail. . . . At a hearing in the court building four weeks later in Bamberg, I escaped through a window in the toilet, went in town, grabbed somebody's bike and escaped to . . . Radelsdorf. . . . My relatives . . . had lived there for decades. During the flight I saw again and again cars coming, probably looking for me. Whenever I saw lights approaching I ducked into the roadside ditch. It was evening in November and it got dark rather early. I waited in the ditch.
  Cars passed, stopped, returned. I knew then they were looking for me!
  About eleven o'clock or twelve I arrived at my relatives. They were quite surprised to see me, that I had escaped. Of course these people were terribly

afraid. If I would be found there, they too would have been arrested. So the first thing they did, they gave me women's clothing. They made a girl out of me—a skirt, a jacket, a turban on my head. . . . In Munchberg . . . I had an uncle. Five o'clock in the morning I was on the way in my lady's clothing on the first workers' train and went on to Bavaria. During the trip, facing me, sat an elderly gentleman who tried to get friendly with me, but I managed to keep him off.

When he finally arrived at his uncle's home, Hans was told again that he could not stay there since it would endanger the family. The uncle sent word to Hans' mother while the boy sought shelter outside the uncle's wagon.

It was cold, very cold, I stayed there until my mother came. . . . She came looking for her child and saved me again. So in my lady's outfit with my mother who did not look like a Gypsy—blond, etc.—we went to Berlin. Again I was hiding out with friends. My mother came every week to Berlin to bring me food. Then I met a German girl with whom I had an affair, and I lived with her. One day this girl said to me, "Last night they put your parents on a truck and took them away. I do not know where." . . . As I learned later, they were taken to Auschwitz.

I was without shelter except for the girl who was hiding me again. I stayed on in Berlin under a false name, had false papers. . . . Now I could not go back to Bernau [my home].

The Nazis had stepped up their actions against the Gypsies. All of them were hounded, and Hans was continually on the run. He discovered two family members in Berlin and the three planned to locate other relatives—either in hiding or in camps—and get them supplies. But on their way from Luxembourg to Belgium, the three boys were picked up by the German police.

They must have gotten a tip. We had stayed in that small town [in Luxembourg] for two weeks and we were strangers, so we were noticed. . . . German police . . . appeared and arrested us. We walked between [them]. . . . During the walking, we said to each other in Romany, our language, "We must run away." At a certain glance all three ran, one to the left, the others to the right, across the railroad tracks, over the hill. We gained some distance, but I lost my way. I ran into a dead end street and there they caught me—two policemen. They threw me down, beat me up, and arrested me. . . . They questioned me about the where and the why. I did not look like a Gypsy. I told them a fairy tale—that I ran away from home, that I wanted to become a soldier, that I wanted to join the SS. They bought that. You know, there were a lot of volunteers in the army and in the SS. Young men had a . . . better chance in uniform. . . . They did not treat me too bad in that jail.

I had again a chance, and again I ran away. Along the street, into a house, up to the attic. . . . I knocked at a door. It was opened—it was a tailor. I will never forget that. I told him the whole story. . . . "Listen," he said, "you stay until it gets dark and then we will . . . get you out of town." . . . The man sewed some rags into my jacket to give me the look of a hunchback, a cane in hand. . . . He showed me how to limp. He took me by the arm and walked me out [of the town].

I walked along the road, but there was one problem. There was a coal mine and every fifteen minutes the glowing coal was brought out and lit up the whole area like daylight. On top of that there was a very strong wind, hindering me in my walk. I could move only very slowly. After about one hour I saw a light. I had to be careful. It could be police. This bicyclist passed. Then two lights approached—a car. I thought, He must have told them. . . . I disappeared into a field, laid on my tummy. It was raining lightly which helped me. The car passed again. I heard dogs, people talking, "He must be here. He cannot be any further." The lights of the coal mine went out again. Apparently the dogs did not have my trail through the rain. I got away from them.

All of a sudden, I found myself standing at the Moselle River. . . . I took off my clothes, tied them up and put them on top of my head, and swam to the other side of the river. This chase went on til six o'clock in the morning. I arrived in Luxembourg in a hotel where we always stayed . . . as actors. I had always some money sewn into my clothes so that in case of danger I could always manage to go on. . . . I gave my soaking wet clothes to the chambermaid to dry and clean and told her to wake me up. . . . The flight continued, but it did not last very long. I had hardly stepped out when the Gestapo stopped me and put me in jail in Luxembourg where I met my two cousins. The questioning started again. . . . Then a transport was assembled. . . . We did not know where to.

Hans, his cousins, and other Gypsies were taken by cattle car to Auschwitz—to the specially designated Gypsy camp in Birkenau.

The first question was, "What are you?" The answer: "Musicians." "So play something for us." He came to me and asked, "What instrument are you playing?" Answer: "I play the harp." "We don't have a harp." The others got a piece of bread. I got nothing.

The Gypsy prisoners were taken into a "political room" where a Polish clerk—a criminal prisoner—registered them. Their clothes were taken away, numbers were tatooed on their arms, heads were shaven. Then, amazingly, Hans was reunited with his family.

I did not recognize my mother. Her hair was cut off. . . . I asked her where the two [youngest] children were. . . . One was one and a half, the other three years old. . . . She told me they were dead.

For a certain time we were permitted to live together in this barrack. . . . My mother . . . my father . . . and [the] six children [who] were still alive. . . . We were all in one bunk with four racks. . . . This was the Gypsy camp. Next to it was the Jewish camp. Next to it was the Czech camp. People were sorted out like goods.

I volunteered for a work detail—night shift, you know. We had to collect the dead from the hospital barrack at night, about seven o'clock, and take them to the crematorium. We had an army truck which we had to pull with straps. The Gypsy camp Birkenau was next to the crematorium. So we collected the dead, threw them off the truck, and they were burnt there. And for that, for the night shift, we got every time an extra ration of one-half a loaf of bread. This bread I saved to give to my mother and my brothers and sisters.

I can never forget that. You see, I am now sixty-two years old. I will be able to forget when I am dead.

Hans' mother contracted typhus.

Mother *had* to leave for the hospital barrack. That was the rule. She was so emaciated that she did not have any strength left in her to live. The next day I visited her and tried to wash her mouth. . . . Typhus is terrible. . . . One looked always for some liquid and liquid was equal to death. I washed her mouth out. She embraced me. It was so sad. . . . Next day she was dead.

And so it went on. . . . One after the other . . . of my brothers and sisters . . . died of starvation . . . My father was beaten severely. He starved to death.

When I also had typhoid fever, I was also taken to the hospital barrack. . . . They made experiments with us. They gave us live typhus injections. . . . Dr. Mengele came one day into the hospital barrack. . . . He took a pretty boy, who had also typhus [but] was on the way to get better. In the middle of the hospital room there was kind of an oven. Sometimes the inmates sat on it or used it to cook some potatoes which they had stolen from the kitchen. He was a beautiful boy, dark-skinned. Dr. Mengele put a white cloth on this oven, put this child on it, bent him over, took a long needle and inserted it in his back, his spine, all the way to the top. I was in my bunk. I was already getting better. The needle broke; he tried to pull it out, but he did not succeed. We were not too distressed to see that because we had seen too much before. . . . The needle was broken off—only about ten centimeters he had pulled out. Some white stuff was oozing out. . . . One of the block doctors took him back to the barrack. A few hours later the child was dead.

The next day on my way to the toilet—you know I had typhus and dysentery [and] if you did not hold your drinking of water, you could not stop. I always

had to pass this "butcher block" on the way to the toilet. Dr. Mengele had added a room of six to eight square meters. There was a runoff in the cement with blood. There was the child. He had it cut open from top to bottom with a saw—like a butcher would cut open an animal. He took the intestines and filled them into jars filled with a clear liquid. These were his "experiments."

After months of illness, starvation, and beatings, Hans was eventually transferred to the labor camp at Flossenberg. Warned that the American troops were advancing, the Nazis evacuated the camp and marched over one thousand inmates from camp to camp under SS guard.

Five of us [in each row], arms linked, we walked [through] woods and meadows. . . . Did you know, one can sleep standing up? We did that to the end. Those who could not make it were shot on the spot. There was a "commando." They were buried on the spot, about one-half meter deep. . . . The American planes were flying overhead. These were not bombers; they were reconnaissance planes. They followed us.

It was one o'clock in the morning. . . . We had heard that [the Nazis] wanted to do us in at the last station [so three of us] ran away. . . . We were hiding in a barn about one kilometer from there. About three, four o'clock in the morning we heard machine-gun fire for about one hour. Later on I learned that all had been shot.

We went into a village and were hiding in a school. There were SS in that village and the village was attacked because the SS defended themselves. I went to the basement and found a long stick and kind of a white sheet, attached it to the stick, and held it out the window. And so we surrendered the village and thus saved the village from being destroyed.

The SS ran away. They caught some SS later. Under their uniforms they wore prison garb. Many of the SS went to the camps . . . and pretended to be inmates, later emigrated.

[As for my family] everybody dead. All of them.

From the testimony of Hans Braun, translated by Hanna Silver

5   *Erica*

---

*Among the thousands of Germans who fled to Holland for safety when
Hitler came to power were Erica and her family. For a few years they
were safe—until the May 1940 invasion of Holland when they were "detained" in Westerbork until they were sent to Bergen-Belsen. Erica spent
most of her teen years in these camps, finding an enhanced Jewish identity
and close support group in the Zionist youth organization at Westerbork.
She chronicled her experiences and reactions in a diary and collection of
poetry. She has translated here for the first time a poem of optimism—
her fear carefully controlled—written the day her family was deported to
Bergen-Belsen.*

*Because they had been born in Germany, Erica's family and 25,000
other Jewish refugees in the Netherlands were considered "stateless" and
were destined for early deportation. Detained first in the transit camp at
Westerbork, established originally by the Dutch authorities for Jewish
refugees and later used by the Germans for deportations to Auschwitz,
Erica's family was fortunate to delay their transfer until February 1944.
An affadavit to join family in Palestine protected them from direct deportation to Auschwitz and instead diverted them to Bergen-Belsen where,
they hoped, time was on their side.*

Erica was born in 1928 in Munich, Germany. Both of her parents came
from families successful in manufacturing and brought their two children
into a world of comfort and culture. They attended a liberal synagogue
and, to Erica, their Jewish identification seemed marginal.

There was emphasis on being German much more than being Jewish. It was
. . . the Emancipation, and you didn't do this because it might be "too Jewish,"
or you didn't do that because it might be "too Jewish."

When Hitler came to power, the family left Germany.

They just felt that once they were out of Germany . . . once they crossed the
border, Hitler's influence would disappear. . . . They knew that in Holland there
was . . . a much more liberal attitude towards religious freedom. . . . The rest of
the family also left . . . to Portugal . . . to South Africa . . . to London . . . to Rho-
desia . . . and they all stopped in Holland . . . and visited with us . . . and then
went on their merry way. . . . But my parents were the least farsighted.

The family moved to Haarlem, a suburb of Amsterdam, next door to
another German Jewish family, and the two fathers started a joint business
venture in Amsterdam.

It was a very pleasant lifestyle. . . . I had never really experienced anti-
Semitism. . . . Kids would say, "Oh, but you are not really Dutch," but not
often. . . . I wanted desperately to be one of them, one of the Dutch. I knew that
I was stateless.[1]
It was nice [but] there was an awful lot of talk all through the years about
what could happen. It was not the greatest feeling of security, no. . . . I don't
think I ever felt terribly secure as a child. I felt secure in the family, that sort
of thing. But I remember ever since I was a little girl there was talk about Hitler
and this could happen, and that could happen. This uncle is leaving and that
uncle is leaving. It was not . . . a settled kind of life.

Erica was eleven years old in June 1940 when Holland suddenly fell
to the Germans, and despite some last minute attempt to get to England,
the family knew that now "we were stuck . . . and things were going to
be very, very different." In September of 1940 the family, tagged as
stateless and under German control, had twenty-four hours to move inland
to Hilversum. There Erica and her brother moved in with their former
housekeeper, a German woman who had cared for them for five years
until she married a German Jew and moved to this small town. She also
secured housing for Erica's parents ten minutes away in a small pension
run by another Jewish family.

---

[1]Refers to person deprived of nationality and citizenship by the Nazis or Nazi-controlled regime.

So, for half a year we lived like that. . . . It was a big change. Once in a while we would eat with our parents, like on a Sunday we would have a meal. . . . Finally, my parents rented a house in this community.

By then I was in seventh grade and it was the first time that I did have an anti-Semitic experience. [I had] a math teacher, a Dutch math teacher, and he failed me for being Jewish. . . . I did all the work . . . but he would always grade me lower than other people who did the same. [But] he was the only one. . . . [The other Dutch people were] wonderful, absolutely wonderful. . . . [When] I brought the star . . . to sew it on my coat . . . I know I didn't feel terrible because a lot of people wore them and a lot of Dutch people put them on. It was sort of a defiant thing.

Erica's awareness of what was happening in the rest of Europe was limited.

I knew about *Kristallnacht*. We did hear about that . . . by radio and by, you know, people telling this. But I truly can't say that I was aware of Polish Jews and Russian Jews and Hungarian Jews. I was not even a teenager at that time.

But in January 1942, the German Jews from Hilversum were deported to Westerbork—called a detention center but really a concentration camp in the northeastern part of Holland where illegal immigrants from Germany, the "old campers," had been sent since 1937. At twenty-four hours notice, Erica and her family stored their possessions with Christian friends. With one suitcase each, they were shipped with about a hundred others by standard passenger train to the camp.

It was in January, and it was very, very cold, and I wore a lot of clothes. I remember my father introduced me . . . to another young girl and she was the same age. . . . Her name was Jo . . . and this was my first friend in the concentration camp. . . . Until this day we're good friends. . . . All the people who had children kept the children [with them] except for two, and it was me and she. And we had to live in the barracks for women because we were just over thirteen.

When we got there, we got food and we were told to register. It was all very orderly and it was not a bit scary. . . . My parents were always worried. . . . I remember that a young man came and he was much older than me. He was twenty or twenty-two years old, so he was really an older man, and he told me that there was a youth group in the camp, and I immediately took a liking to him. . . . He did have a youth group, and I thought it was going to be great fun and it was. It was great fun! Can you believe?

The first half year [before the deportations started] . . . was really not bad. I lived in this barrack with women but I ate at my parents'. They had a room in a . . . long barrack divided into two-room apartments and then finally moved into another barrack where we had a bigger room and we [were all] in this one room. . . . You got food rations and from that you could . . . do your own cooking, and also we got fed from the camp. . . . We had our own hospital . . . Jewish doctors. . . . We had our own orchestra. . . . You could still go to Amsterdam once in awhile [because the Dutch were still in charge of the camp]. . . . I got permission to go for a weekend to Amsterdam . . . and then I went back to the concentration camp. . . . In the first half year [I went to school]. It was in German, because the kids who had lived there for several years had all come from Germany and they didn't know much Dutch. . . . It was in a little schoolhouse . . . and I remember we had . . . some English lessons.

In the youth group, Erica experienced something new in her education.

I was not brought up with any kind of religious background. I had gone to Sunday School to learn a little bit and I had gone to the synagogue once in a while, but [this] was much more Orthodox-oriented than I'd ever been exposed to . . . much more traditional Judaism. . . . The youth group met on Saturday afternoon. . . . We used to do a lot of *hora*[2] dancing and we used to have a lot of intellectual discussions. . . . We studied the holidays and we observed the holidays and we prayed and it was really, you know—it was the works. . . . I loved it. . . . I felt tremendous. I mean this really gave me a lot of strength.

Then in July 1942, deportations from Westerbork started.

Things changed drastically. Suddenly the men were called from whatever they were doing to build barracks because we were told more people were coming. And they did come—in droves.

[One] group that was sent . . . to Auschwitz [were] orphans from Utrecht—German-born orphans. . . . I was for awhile in the women's barrack with [them]. . . . It was a very nice group and again they were all brought up very Orthodox and I learned [more about Judaism] when I associated with them. I was considered part of the group because I wasn't living at home. This group, as a unit, was all sent to Auschwitz. And that was my first realization. . . . We knew they were being sent to something horrible but we didn't know what it was. . . . You might get killed on the way. You might get starved. You might get beaten to death. You might be tortured. But . . . we didn't know that Auschwitz had gas chambers. . . . I never knew that. Nobody knew that.

Every week, Tuesday and Friday, people were sent to Auschwitz. Every week people would come in—in masses and masses and masses—and the next Tuesday, half of them or three-quarters of them would be shipped out. . . . The se-

[2] An Israeli dance.

lection was made simply if they had no papers to show that they were sponsored [that is, that they could officially go to another country], that they had the passport of Paraguay [for example]. . . . You could buy a passport from South American countries. Many Jews did that. . . . We had our own little papers. . . . We had an affidavit to go to Israel that an aunt in Israel sent. . . . That saved us, too.

After the transports started, the schools in Westerbork closed. Since Erica was over thirteen she was required to work. "We felt that time was on our side, because the longer you were in Westerbork, the better off you were." Fortunately she was able to get a job as a lab technician under the supervision of a friend.

She was from Vienna and she was very charming. As a matter of fact, she got married in Westerbork. I was at the wedding and one of [my] poems . . . is about them getting married. . . . I was able to get a job in the lab that she was heading, and I was trained to be a lab technician. I learned to do urine analysis, and I learned to do blood testing, and after awhile I would go around the hospital and take blood from the patient's finger, and to think that I was able to do that at fourteen seems, of course, quite amazing.

But her job was under the shadow of the Tuesday and Friday deportations.

I did, at one point . . . get up . . . at four in the morning because a friend was to be shipped to Auschwitz, and he was alone. . . . I was very, very fond of him and I brought him food to take on this trip and I did see him. . . . There was a railroad track that ran right into [the camp]. . . . Most of the time the trains were not regular trains with windows. These were cattle cars. . . . Yes, we were petrified.

I'm sure they all thought about [escaping] but, you see, the camp was surrounded with very high barbed wire fences, and there were outposts all over with Germans and machine guns.

I had my prayerbook and I used to say my prayers and I used to remember all of the people that I had been with. By then, most of them had been killed in Auschwitz. But I didn't know that.

For Erica and her family, their time came on February 15, 1944, when they were shipped to Bergen-Belsen, a six- to seven-hour ride in a passenger train.

We were selected to go to Belsen because we had . . . the affidavit for Israel. . . . Belsen was a camp where they had all . . . sorts of exceptions. . . . It was not

all Jewish. There were Polish criminals, there were Gypsies, there was a section
of Hungarian Jews. . . . [There were] Jews . . . from Tripoli and Africa. . . . We
were in a Jewish section and top dogs in that section were . . . Greek Jews from
Salonica. . . . Why? Because they were there first. . . . You had to speak French
. . . because the Greeks were in charge and they spoke Ladino[3] and they spoke
Greek and many of them spoke French.

This was a very international section of Belsen. They did not have gas chambers. They had work commandos. . . . At one point, I was in charge of children
in day care centers. . . . People had little children and mothers would work and
we were baby sitters. . . . At another point in time I was in a factory. We made
some sort of material for the war effort, for the Germans. It was plastic piping
that had to be woven in a certain way.

The barracks were lousy. . . . [There were] triple deckers. It got so crowded
that you had to have two in a bed. At one point there was a lot of disease because
of lice and a lot of people had [typhus]. I [also had] typhoid twice. . . . I also
had jaundice. I had that twice.

There wasn't much family life. . . . You did get together for meals once in
awhile. . . . Every day we would have turnips, once a day. We did get some
soup, the second meal, and in the morning, some sort of coffee substitute. . . .
It was sanitary to a certain degree. We went to bathhouses and they would turn
on the water and you took showers, hot water, and this was maybe once every
so often. . . . Toilets were outhouses. But they had bathrooms with sinks and
you could wash there. But I remember very often in the coldest winter months
that we would use the coffee [to] wash ourselves because it was hot.

They attempted to continue the Jewish youth group of Westerbork.

But it wasn't as often. It wasn't as nice. I know one group who would make
little matzos for Passover. They got . . . flour and water and they would make
little matzos over the fire. . . . There were no services . . . not that I know of.

Erica's grandparents were in Westerbork and Bergen-Belsen as well,
and she recalls that her grandmother did not have to attend morning roll
call because of her age.

I remember very clearly that I, on a very cold morning, hid under her covers
not to go outside and a SS came in and pulled the covers from her and there I
was. And he could have done all sorts of things, and I just gave him a little
smile and said that I wouldn't do it anymore and he let me go. But that was
pretty risky. But then, you did a lot of things that were pretty risky.

[3]The mixed Spanish and Hebrew dialect spoken by Sephardic Jews.

Toward the end of the war the danger from bombing attacks increased for the prisoners as for civilians.

We had a lot of bombardments around the area. Not in the camp, although at one point a British plane strayed and did hit the camp a little bit. It killed one woman and she was standing next to me. Next to me. . . . She was hit and I was not.

In April 1945, the Belsen prisoners were put on a forced march of seven kilometers to reach a train that would take them to Auschwitz. Sick with para-typhoid, Erica doubted that she could make it.

There were several hundred of us German Jews, Dutch Jews, French Jews . . . Greek Jews. . . . We walked the seven kilometers and reached a . . . train [of] cattle cars. . . . It was a whole conglomeration of people. . . . I remember sitting on the platform before going in [the train] and it was the only time all these years that I broke down and cried and sobbed and I thought I would never make it. But I got on the train. . . . I was so tired and I thought that it was the end. I figured that was it.

It was a horrendous ride. From April 7 or 9 until April 23 on the train. Every day we would be attacked by planes, or there would be alarms and we had to hide. . . . On the way to Berlin we were in the middle of the river and there was an alarm and we couldn't go back and we couldn't go forward, and we were told, this was it, guys, and I remember saying the *Sh'ma Yisroel.*[4] But we made it. . . . We left the train in certain places . . . because we had to find food. We ate raw potatoes, we ate whatever we could get. . . . We were in one town where, suddenly, there was an alarm again and everybody had to get out of the cars and I lost my family and I ran and hid under a locomotive and then I thought, this is stupid, and I ran away. And just as I was running away, maybe a hundred yards, the whole locomotive was hit and it blew up.

This was the thirteenth or fourteenth day and the train stopped. It was early in the morning, and we could see the Germans. We were not many by then. . . . Many of them died. . . . They had white flags and two Russian soldiers appeared on horses. And that was the liberation. And we couldn't understand them and they couldn't understand us, but we knew we were free.

The Soviet soldiers indicated that the liberated prisoners should go to Tröbitz, the closest town, to find food and housing.

We were told the Germans would leave or they would make room for us. . . . I didn't have to displace—they moved downstairs and they gave us the upstairs

---

[4]Hear, O Israel—the watchword of the Jewish faith.

... willingly, because they knew if they didn't they were going to be shot [by the Russians].... We found a German abandoned army train with enormous supplies of food, especially cheese, and we practically all got sick because it was too much. After that, a lot of us got typhoid, and even though we had been innoculated, evidently we weren't strong enough at this point and many people died right after being liberated.... The Russians set up a hospital and they gave excellent care.... [My whole family] was very sick.... I took care of everybody and then I got it. And then two Russian soldiers wanted to come and take me with them and I said, "Typhoid! Typhoid!" and that... scared them off. But, otherwise, I am sure, they would have taken me to rape me. But they didn't.

The family returned to Holland by July 1945 and Erica left to study in the United States one year later.

I am a great optimist by nature, and I feel that even throughout this horrendous experience, had it not been for my strong hope, I would never have made it. I do look for good things in any situation [and] there were some snips of it that were definitely good ... wonderful people ... interesting things ... joyful things.... Some of the things in Westerbork, as crazy as it sounds, they were good for me in a certain way—not that I was in Westerbork, but some of the connections that I made, and the experiences I had.

* * *

This poem was written by me on the day I left Westerbork to be transported to Bergen-Belsen. The original copy was given to my friends of the youth group to which I belonged. I copied the poem in one of the two small notebooks in which I had written poems in Westerbork and later in Bergen-Belsen. This covered a three and a half year period. I held on to the notebooks and they are very precious to me. This is the first time I have translated a poem. I was fifteen years old when I wrote this poem in German.

Farewell Poem
15 February 1944

When I leave you today
At the last moment I'd like to say
That I want to write a short letter to you
Because write you I must, that's true.
I want to thank you, everyone
For all that you've given me
And will remain grateful to you
As long as I hope my life will be.
It was really always so sweet

Because we all felt so connected
Yet now we have to separate
Few will remain here, it's suspected.
Now that I am departing from here
And perhaps won't see you in many a year
I wish you all the best; may things go well for you
Stay strong as iron; hold on to your courage, too.
We'll do the same; oh, alright let it be
Who knows, before long each other we'll see.
Perhaps in Eretz,[5] or America
Perhaps in Asia, or in Africa.
To reunite in Eretz would be so great
That would be wonderful, oh, what a beautiful fate.
I shall also remain brave
And help in every way there
And continue our work
Which can be done no matter where.
We hope soon the war's end will arrive
Then for better times all of us shall strive
So we can learn and a goal into focus we'll bring
So we can be jubilant and joyously we'll sing
Because in G-d we trust, there will be a tomorrow
He always is there to help us in our sorrow.
When there's trust in us all
And on G-d in faith we call
Then we can certainly go our separate ways
We hope and we know we'll meet in happier days.
Until then we must remember one another
We must continue to work and brave we must be
May G-d give that we soon greet each other anew
In Eretz, in our youth group, you and me.
   So *shalom, lehitraot*[6]
   Think of your *chavera*[7]
   Who also thinks of you,
   Her name is Erika.

Erica Herz Van Adelsberg
March 20, 1988
Philadelphia, Pennsylvania

From the testimony of Erica Herz Van Adelsberg

[5]*Eretz Yisroel* or land of Israel.
[6]Good-bye, au revoir.
[7]Friend (f.).

6   *Ernst*

Ernst was twelve when the Germans bombed Rotterdam and fourteen when his family was deported to the Westerbork concentration camp in Holland and later to Bergen-Belsen in Germany. From an adult vantage point, he questions why his father was reluctant to take advantage of opportunities to get his family to safety while there was still a chance. Ernst also recalls times where he could have escaped alone and decided against it. And at times, methods of survival in the concentration camp took precedence over previous standards of behavior. Throughout Ernst's recollection is his ongoing struggle to understand these choices.

Ernst came from an assimilated Dutch Jewish family which was comfortable in the religious and cultural liberalism of Western Europe. The native Christian population had generally accepted their Jewish neighbors before the war and protested Nazi persecution of the Jews in their valiant resistance to the German invasion and occupation. But Germans gained complete control of the Netherlands in the spring of 1940 and effectively carried out their plans for deportation of all Dutch Jews. Out of approximately 125,000, fewer than 20,000 survived.

Ernst was the youngest of three sons of an upper-middle-class merchant family in Rotterdam. They lived comfortably within the general Dutch community and Ernst recalls no anti-Semitism in his public school. In May 1940, Nazis overran Holland after severe bombardments and occupied the country. It was just before Ernst's twelfth birthday.

I have some very vivid recollections of that bombing, because we lived through it. . . . Everywhere it knocked out windows in spite of the fact that we had taped them. The streets were literally so littered with glass that one was walking on glass all the time. Amazingly none of us were seriously injured.

A bomb fell outside of our house a block up and our house caught on fire because of it. An entire block up in flames. . . . There was a very fine villa, with a thatched roof and it was in a little park where there was a pond, and the thatched roof was burning. People were carrying all sorts of valuables out of the house. . . . The water system had been bombed and there was no pressure in the lines. . . . And here was this other man and I was only yet a boy, manning a pump, to pump water out of the pond to . . . spray water on the house.

I remember . . . there was a very fine liquor store and in fear of German soldiers coming and drinking alcohol and going absolutely wild . . . every bottle in the shop was smashed. . . . The floor of the place was literally filled with wine and liquor. You could stand there and could smell it. . . . There was street fighting for two, three days . . . because the Dutch army put up a very good defense. . . . And so we were in the middle of all this.

We thought of fleeing south. My father had a car and the reason that we didn't—and now it seems to foolish—was my father said, ''Well, I don't have enough money on me. I have to go to the bank and get money, but the banks are closed and there is no way to get money.'' Of course, we would have just got into the car and fled south. We might have been able to get to Spain. Well, we didn't do this. We stayed put.

There was also a chance for Ernst's older brother to escape, but, again, his father felt that staying put was the safest choice. This brother, who had graduated from high school, had been studying with a chemist who was also an officer in the Dutch army and had underground contacts.

He had offered my brother a chance to stay in England. . . . Planes used to land at night . . . in northern Holland . . . and pick up people, and my brother was given the chance to escape. My father would have none of this. In those early days, he felt that it was too dangerous. Later on, of course, he deeply regretted this.

Shortly after this, the family moved to a smaller apartment elsewhere in the city.

I don't know why we moved, whether it was somewhat cheaper in rent or our apartment had been too damaged, but I was too young to be told that.

The Nazis segregated the Jews from the non-Jews.

At first we continued to go to public school. . . . In 1941 . . . it was forbidden . . . for Jewish children to go to public school . . . following the Nazi policy in

Germany where Jewish schools had been set up. These were copies of the public school [but] all the students were Jewish and all the faculty was Jewish. . . . We met in a barn building . . . around which there was nothing. . . . I'll never forget that year because it was in many ways a stimulating year. . . . We had an outstanding faculty. . . . Jewish children from all over Rotterdam had to go to that one high school. . . . Naturally, since I was going to school with other Jewish children, my friends were now mainly Jewish.

Ernst's religious tutoring continued in Nazi-occupied Holland, and in 1941 he had his Bar Mitzvah. Since the synagogue his family had attended had been destroyed by the bombing, the ceremony was held in the small chapel of the Jewish old age home.

By 1942, the Dutch Jews had to wear the yellow star, travel restrictions were imposed, and Ernst's family's financial security was shaken.

My father had his office at his house although he had a . . . wholesale warehouse which was separate. . . . Suddenly a man arrived at our door . . . who informed us that he had been appointed by the German authorities as trustee of my father's business. . . . I remember my father's panic. . . . He still tried to carry on, but once the trustee had been appointed, he really was no longer very much in charge.

[In] our gradually restricting circle of life . . . my father sold his car. . . . The car . . . I think a 1938 Chevrolet . . . [meant] a great deal to me . . . being a boy . . . but he felt that he could no longer use it. Gasoline, of course, was one of the things that were restricted. Anyway, he sold it.

And now . . . I remember my father came home in a terrible panic because there had been some sort of roundup of Jewish young men. . . . This now put panic, fear into our lives. . . . There were also then, I do know this, rumors that we would be deported . . . to Poland. And I remember very specifically my father saying, "I will never allow this to happen to us." And as a result, and I did participate in this, we began to make plans with Christian friends, and we had some contact apparently with the underground, that we would flee. We would take what might be called an underground train to Switzerland. We were going to take the train to south of Holland to Brabant. We would bicycle across the Belgian frontier. We would go through Belgium into northern France. The *Maquis*[1] would somehow get us . . . into Switzerland. . . . My father had accumulated some money and we had made contacts . . . some contacts through this individual [the chemist who had offered to help his brother]. We had planned in August of 1942 to make a run for it. It was dangerous. We were aware of this. [But] we would be aided. . . . We had plans.

[1]French underground.

But during the second week of August his parents were summoned to the Rotterdam police headquarters.

This, I don't need to tell you, is a very unusual thing, because as law-abiding Dutch citizens we never had any contact with the police. . . . My parents went together and in the afternoon my father came back alone. My mother had been arrested and been held in prison.

It's quite incredible. About two houses down from us . . . lived the inspector of police. He turned out to be a Nazi. And he observed that my mother had some groceries delivered to her house and this was illegal. This is something that she had done all her life as a housewife. [This was] a normal practice in Europe before World War II [but] in the early summer of 1942, the hours to shop for groceries were restricted [for Jews] and . . . home deliveries of groceries . . . was also forbidden. . . . She had called as usual to order something . . . forgetting that it was no longer allowed and the manager . . . had probably said that this was an old customer . . . for maybe fifteen years . . . and had not paid attention. . . . As good law-abiding citizens . . . we had registered as Jews . . . in 1940 . . . one of the first acts of . . . the German occupation authorities. . . . Terrible mistake. Of course, now, hindsight. So we were listed, we were known as Jews. . . . My mother was kept arrested [and] this meant, of course, that we were now caught.

About four weeks later, the police informed the family that they could be reunited if they accompanied Ernst's mother to Westerbork, a camp in northeastern Holland. The first round of Dutch deportations had just started.

The Dutch post office sent notices to people, and there were some Jewish families living around us who were then informed by mail that they had to arrive at a certain date, with only that which they could carry, at a collection center and they would be put on a train to Westerbork. But we were a special case. I never did quite find out why. Anyway, on the twenty-fourth of August 1942, we all came to the Dutch police station. . . . We were united with my mother and the next morning we were put under special guard on the train . . . a regular scheduled train to Utrecht. . . . As a matter of fact, looking back on it, when we changed trains in Utrecht, they were so lax that if I had run away, I could have easily escaped. I could have managed without any difficulty to run away.

The family stayed in the hands of the Dutch police until they arrived at Westerbork where they passed into German control.

It was very early in the whole process of deportation. And the first thing that was done in Westerbork, I remember that, was to build a railroad through . . .

so the trains could come right into the camp. . . . Westerbork became . . . a transit [point]. . . . We managed to hold on, to hang on, to stay in Westerbork from August 1942 until February 1944 and we saw, in fact, virtually the entire Dutch-Jewish community pass before us, including some of our relatives, including my eighty-three-year-old grandfather.

Shortly after their arrival, Ernst's mother became ill and was transferred to a university hospital outside of the camp where she remained during their years in Westerbork. Ernst still questions whether this was one of the possible reasons for their staying in the camp as long as they did without being deported to Poland.

My mother all of this time maybe pulled some strings there . . . and that was one way that we managed to hang on. . . . And there were other ways. Because we arrived so early in Westerbork, all of us got jobs there in the camp bureaucracy. . . . My father became . . . the manager of one of the barracks. . . . I became a messenger boy, but I had a marvelous title and even an arm band. . . . In the process we became very well known in the camp. We made, of course, connections, political connections. . . . I ran messages and I was all over the camp. I knew when a new transport was arriving. I knew when a train came in [or] that a train would go to the East. . . . Gradually, as these transports became systematized and the railroad spur had been built, . . . it amounted to a thousand people a week that were sent on the train [and] the SS became more prominent in the administration of the camp. Nevertheless, security [in the camp] was fairly lax. And, I remember once or twice being sent out of the camp to a nearby place outside the barbed wire, and I just walked out and was not stopped. Again I could have escaped but it never occurred to me. Perhaps because we felt fairly secure. . . . Once [we were allowed to visit my mother]. That involved a two to three hour bus trip. . . . We could have [escaped] but I think we probably went under some sort of escort. . . . I was, of course, young. I spoke, of course, the language [but], I mean, to leave somehow the family? . . . If I had been older, more organized, if I would have known what was in store. . . .

Ernst recalls an "assembly," a line-up of prisoners addressed by the camp commandant, Gemmeker.

I don't quite know the purpose of why the people were standing there [but] people tried not so much to protest as to argue that they should not be deported. . . . While I heard this, the significance of this *never* made an impact on me. This was 1942–3—general knowledge of Auschwitz and the execution and gassing of people was not known. . . . If there would have been knowledge of what really happened to people in Poland I suspect that there would have been far more protest. People went on the whole peaceably. They thought we were being resettled. I remember one group of young Zionists marching to the train to be deported and singing the *Hatikvah*.

This false sense of security did not remove the current anguish but did encourage them to think it was temporary.

I also remember very distinctly in September 1942 Rosh Hashana and Yom Kippur services in Westerbork which were held in the barracks, where we were surrounded by iron bedsteads, two and three high, and that either my brothers or my father said, ''Well, this is one High Holiday service that we won't forget.''

Ernst describes the organization of Jewish prisoners, citing the wide range of its involvement in camp life.

We organized a theatre group and we put on a cabaret—Cabaret Westerbork. I still have the program. . . . There were some very fine Jewish actors, not all of them Dutch. As a matter of fact, the entire text was in German and the commander . . . and all came and thought it was terrific and applauded and sat in the front row. And there was lots of, you know, good cabaret humor. . . . It was a way to keep alive.

At the other extreme, the central committee of this organization was involved in the deportation process—dispensing forms, hearing appeals, and, finally, making the painful decisions which would satisfy the German quotas.

My father worked for the organization, but he was only on the barracks level. He was not on the central committee. He would have avoided that because he did not want to take responsibility. It was obvious to us that certain decisions had to be taken, but to him it was obvious that he would have found them morally unacceptable. So, he kept himself at a low profile.

I have copies of that form . . . you had to sign [when] the Germans gave the opportunity to Jews who wished to avoid deportation . . . by allowing themselves to be sterilized, through surgery, through an operation.

Ernst and his family could maintain some contact outside the camp— sending letters, receiving food parcels—and radios in the camp provided news of the war. But Ernst's memories of these events are vague or, as he recalls, viewed with disinterest.

I was still fairly young. I was fourteen or fifteen and the political news didn't interest us that much. Or at least me. . . . I never went to school. There were several [attempts] to organize a school in the camp, but that failed, and I was then too free and too wild. . . . I knew my way around the camp. . . . And, let me say, too, that while food was not plentiful in Westerbork, it was sufficient, and I will admit [and] am not ashamed that I became one of the specialists finding food or plainly stealing it. I was very good at going into the kitchen in the food supply and managing to scare up extra rations. . . . I was something of a wild devil. I took all sorts of chances especially in finding my way around, and literally, to use the word of the time, "liberating" food supplies. . . . One should make a study of what the relaxation of standards and civilized behavior does on the young people.

Ernst's mother was sent back to Westerbork from the hospital by early February 1944 "and this was probably an indication that our days were now numbered." But Ernst's father and some business contacts were able to arrange the family's transfer to a "special camp."

My father had been an importer and exporter. . . . He had done business with England [and] if the Germans won the war we could be exchanged for furniture. Apparently the Germans had bought this idea that he was a fairly important businessman and could be exchanged for furniture. How we got on that list, how we managed this, I do not know, but it was achieved. . . . We were sent on a special train to Bergen-Belsen . . . in February . . . 1944.

Bergen-Belsen was a special complex of camps for prisoners of particular designation. Through his father's efforts, Ernst and his family had not been deported "to the East," to Auschwitz, but they still found Bergen-Belsen a drastic change from Westerbork.

The conditions were much harsher . . . barracks with wooden beds . . . food was much more limited and the work was much harder. . . . The first work . . . was dig an enormous pit which was apparently meant for a septic tank . . . that may well have been later on used for a grave, a mass grave. I don't know. We also had to push railway lorries up a small track . . . to carry sand or gravel. . . . I was then assigned to what is known as the shoe battalion. . . . There was literally a mountain of old shoes. It must have been at least ten or fifteen feet high and this was part of the German effort to save resources. . . . I don't think they were shoes from Auschwitz. . . . I'm pretty sure that they had simply been collected all over Germany. . . . We sat in a tent at long benches and we took those shoes apart, the nails, the cardboard, the leather, whatever. . . . Each piece was put in barrels . . . and I'm sure that the products were usable in the economy at war. They were very short of raw materials. So, I must say, I'm afraid, that I contributed to the German war effort.

Ernst took on a heavy detail of unloading freight trains in order to get a little more food, and the physical exertion and inadequate diet took their toll.

[But] my father did not do any major work. It was discovered in the camp . . . that he had tuberculosis. One of the reasons for this is, I'm now convinced, that he ate entirely too little and gave most of his food to us. . . . [Also] my oldest brother Hans began to get very ill. . . . He became partly paralyzed. He had to walk with a cane. . . . He had a badly infected hand. He didn't do much work. He did one type of work that we discovered later. He wrote poetry which has been published in Holland. . . . He was twenty-three years old. He must have suffered spiritually and mentally very much. It is obvious from his poetry. He was obviously more aware. Maybe I was a tougher character. Maybe because I was so young, I was simply not conscious of things yet. But I somehow managed to keep going. My middle brother also managed to somehow hang on, although both he and I had one night a very bad experience. . . . I can't even remember why. The guards said we ought to be punished. We had done something wrong. . . . We had spoken when [we] shouldn't have been talking, something. . . . We were told to stand with our noses against the barbed wire at the fence . . . for several hours until the guard came along and told us to go. . . . Somehow, we both managed to keep on going.

By the fall of 1944, sanitary conditions in the camp deteriorated. Lice infestation and typhoid fever became rampant.

We all became sick. . . . There was no way to get the fever down because we didn't have any medication. I apparently was very ill. There were apparently whole weeks that I was not even rational. I could really block it out. I do not remember anything. I [only] remember my mother coming to visit me once with a little extra food. That is a vague recollection. . . . One of the things that . . . stands in my mind . . . was a terrible thing: my mother had long hair and it became impossible to keep it clean and she too became infected and her head had to be shaved. . . . Somehow I did survive the typhoid fever and I had it at least twice, maybe three times. . . . In November, I remember that my father came to tell me that my oldest brother could not fight the infection and . . . had died, which, of course, broke him completely.

In either December or January [1945] . . . I finally threw off the fever and I was allowed to get out of bed. I was in some sort of sick ward. But when I got out of bed I fell on the floor because I had absolutely no strength left. My legs wouldn't carry me. And I literally had to learn how to walk again. . . . I had to go up three steps into a barrack and . . . I couldn't negotiate it. I had to crawl. In the first month of 1945 my parents were still alive and my middle brother was still alive. And now the camp was becoming terribly overcrowded. More and more people being added, not just to our camp . . . but in the prisoner of war camp. People began to die like flies and the [sight] that you may have seen in photographs, I saw with my own eyes— people stacked up . . . row upon row. Moreover, I know that in Bergen-Belsen certain dying prisoners . . . prisoners of war . . . were given gasoline injections. . . . It will kill you after agony of several hours. Apparently this was some sort of crude experimentation. I remember one specific incident when my brother and I were watching where two prisoners in the prisoner of war camp said the prayers of the dead over their dead comrades.

Finally in February or March 1945, the camp was bombed by the British Air Force. Why? We don't know. But several barracks caught on fire; several people got killed. [Then] in April we were taken in trucks—my father, my mother, my brother and I—we were still together . . . and put on a . . . very old train. . . . I would call it a fifth class railroad passenger. Wooden benches, very old. And the train began to move but we did not know where. What apparently the intention was, was to destroy the entire train, with people in it. We were taken by locomotive. Sometimes we sat on a siding for a few hours [and] the locomotive disappeared. The train got bombed or machine-gunned . . . the British or Americans . . . thinking . . . that it was an ammunition train, and we tied some white bedsheets to the top of the train to indicate that it was not. We got to the River Elbe. We were on a bridge, we went over the bridge. The bridge blew up. The plan had apparently been to blow us up on the bridge but the detonation didn't go off in time.

We continued to go and we arrived eventually in Berlin . . . to the suburbs of Berlin [and] we continued in the southeasterly direction. . . . A typhoid epidemic raged on the train and people were dying and as the train moved we used to throw corpses off the train. . . . What can one do?

One night we stopped and the locomotive disappeared and [in the] morning we came out and there was a soldier standing there that we did not recognize— in a different color coat with a rifle and a fur hat. . . . The Russians told us to get off the train immediately. They needed it for their war effort and they told us, "You see Tröbitz there. Go into that village and occupy it. Throw the Germans out of their house. It's yours." It was very easy [to do this]. . . . It's hard to describe . . . but the Germans knew that we were suddenly no longer prisoners.

By now my mother was very weak and my father was weak and I found a little cart and I literally, on the cart, took them into Tröbitz. Now at least we had a decent place to live but we had no food. . . . I remember getting my hands on a bicycle and going to various farmhouses in the little villages nearby and I managed to get a chicken, but then, going on the road back, I ran into some Russians . . . forced labor, who were now free . . . and they stole my bicycle. Easy come, easy go.

But unfortunately now the typhoid epidemic, the "fever" as we called it, had got to my parents, and in fact infested the whole village. Everybody was sick, including the Germans who lived there. . . . What the Russians did simply was to isolate the whole village and give us aspirins. My mother died. . . . My father was then also very ill, and I was ill again. The Russians came in and took my father and [me] to some sort of hospital where my father died.

"On the eighteenth of June, I remember, because this was my father's birthday," Ernst and his brother started a long journey back to Holland, helped by the American army and the Red Cross.

I had no desire to stay in Holland. . . . [When] the American consulate opened in Rotterdam . . . I went immediately to register to emigrate. In the meantime I had started school in the second grade of high school but I really didn't fit in at all. I was too old. I was now seventeen and my whole wartime experience, my whole outlook [had changed]—I can now . . . see . . . looking back. . . . Not wishing to be restrained by any Dutch schoolmaster or classroom . . . I quit school after no more than a month or two.

Fortunately Ernst's visa came through to join his aunt and uncle in California.

Immediately after the war in 1945, we used to talk about nothing else [but our experiences]. And you used to meet people in Rotterdam and Amsterdam that went through so much hurt. I apparently talked about nothing else and people didn't want to hear about it. I did not understand. Maybe I was much too young. I can understand now. You want to forget.

[But] in the immediate post-war period [in America], the universities were full of veterans from World War II who were very motivated to make something of themselves . . . and [then] I wanted to make something of myself. I had to study. . . . If I had stayed in Europe, I would either have died of tuberculosis or I would have turned into a criminal element. I am sure of it. . . . That was the only way to survive. There were very few restraints or moral guides except the one of survival from World War II.

The great luck to me was that I not just left Holland but I left Europe, and I went to an entirely different world. . . . I made such a completely clean break, and from then on, I began to almost be born again. I did not go back to Europe until 1958. For twelve years I did not even have any contact with Europeans. . . . I had finished my studies and had a doctorate degree. . . . I was a very different person who went back to Europe and had then some perspective.

From the testimony of Ernst L. Presseisen

7   *Hanna*

Wanting to protect their fourteen-year-old daughter from danger, Hanna's parents sent her from their home in Prague in 1939 to work on a farm in Denmark. Hanna was confident that they would be reunited after the war. Secure in her privileged social background and anticipating adventure with her friends on the transport, she was unprepared for the hard work, isolation, and devastating news from home that followed. These experiences forced her to draw on inner strength to grow up before she had time to unravel her teenage years.

Czechoslovakia ceased to exist as a nation in 1939, seven months before Hanna was able to leave. The eastern part became a new puppet state called Slovakia and the western part became a Nazi-controlled protectorate. The Czechoslovakian people suffered greatly under the Nazis and 240,000 out of 315,000 Czech Jews (as of 1939) perished.

About 1,500 Jews from Czechoslovakia, Austria, and Germany were able to find refuge in neutral Denmark before the German invasion in April 1940. The liberal Danish government made no distinction between these stateless refugees and the native-born Jews and protected them both from the threat of deportation for over three years. When the Nazis decided to deport the Jews in Denmark in September 1943, the Danes resisted. Moreover, the German military commander in Denmark refused to assign troops to assist in the roundup. The Swedish government provided refuge and, in an astounding humanitarian effort, most of the Jews in Denmark were saved.

Born in the mid 1920's, the daughter of a Prague physician, Hanna grew up in a comfortable, close-knit family unit. They attended synagogue on the High Holidays and otherwise moved in the cultural and professional assimilation of inter-war Prague Jewry. In the fifth grade, she attended a private French school, which, combined with her daily use of German, distinguished her family as part of the upper class.

But on the fringe of this acceptance were some underlying worries:

I do not recall that somebody would personally accost me or be vengeful to me because I was Jewish . . . [but] as a child I remember I always thought if somebody calls me "dirty Jew" or another word, don't say anything. Don't make waves. Take it. If somebody spilled ink on you or put your pigtails into the inkwell behind you because you were, maybe, Jewish . . . don't speak out.

Ironically, this undercurrent moved Hanna toward a stronger Jewish identification than her parents. When she was ten years old she joined the Zionist youth movement.

In school you didn't have sports. . . . So, of course, your parents always looked out that . . . their children didn't develop [only] the brain. . . . There was a sports organization in Czechoslovakia which was called Sokol [which] did not accept Jews like [some] country clubs here, but the Jewish people had their own gyms, and that was called Maccabi. We used to go there after school. . . . There were blue and white shorts that we used to wear. . . . I got caught up in it and I went to camp and had really the pioneer spirit. . . . We slept on the floor and ate from the same pot for five weeks and I was with *chalutzim*[1] all the time. And I stuck with this and my parents were very unhappy about that. And they asked me all the time, "Where are you going?" "I'm going to a meeting here and there." "And who is going to be there?"[This was] the first time I really broke loose. . . . I didn't pay that much attention to how heart-broken they were, but they were certainly not very supportive. . . . Yes, I found my niche . . . and thanks to that I really am here. . . . As a matter of fact, most of my friends who survived, who are in Israel, are from that era.

Hanna's parents tried to shield her from some of the early anti-Jewish measures in Czechoslovakia.

The maid just left. We were told as kids that we were big enough. We don't need a maid. But there were other factors.

In 1938 . . . my Aunt Helena with her family . . . escaped from Vienna and they came to live with us. . . . They were telling us how things [were there] and,

Chalutz (s.), *chalutzim* (pl.), young Zionist pioneer.

of course, everybody was saying that it can happen in Austria but never, never in Czechoslovakia.

In our neighborhood there were a lot of strange Jewish people coming in suddenly, and the streets were more crowded . . . mostly from Austria [and] Poland. . . . When Sudentenland was occupied and there was a general mobilization . . . we had to go to the country [and get] gas masks . . . and we had all these exercises—gas alarms instead of fire alarms, . . . how to go under the desks in the classroom. . . . They thought the city was going to be bombed. . . . That was not a "Jewish Question." It was just a question that the war was coming on.

In the Zionistic organization a [representative] came from Palestine and was telling us what was going to happen and I came home and my parents were saying that it's propaganda and they all want you to go to Palestine. [They told me] nothing is going to happen. [The Zionists] just paint the whole thing black in order to get the young people into Palestine.

[But] my parents let me go . . . in summer 1938 . . . to the training [in] a *hachshara* camp [in preparation for Palestine]. We really lived a *chalutz* life and I loved it. . . . We studied the whole political situation [and] I learned Hebrew . . . to the chagrin of my parents since they were studying . . . French.

In March 1939, Czechoslovakia was occupied by the Germans and was renamed the Protectorate Bohemia-Moravia. Shortly after this,

when I got to school the whole school was full of German troops. They eliminated the French school and they used it as the headquarters and . . . they said that we are going to have classrooms somewhere else . . . except for the Jewish students. The Jewish students could not attend. . . . [But] there was Jewish school . . . right away. Young men of seventeen and eighteen . . . became teachers. . . . I didn't want to go. I was just going to the Zionist movement [but] my brother . . . attended the Jewish school. . . . He was extremely brilliant. . . . He wrote a lot of poetry when he was only like ten or eleven years old. . . . He started a newspaper. . . . He drew beautiful cartoons. He was talented, very talented.

Hanna's parents began to see the danger around them.

There were . . . a lot of clandestine meetings in our house. I think they were trying to get to Uganda. . . . They tried to get papers and get to America . . . but nothing was moving out of America. Papers were not coming. . . . The wheels were grinding too slowly to save many people.

Hanna's last summer in Czechoslovakia was spent at her camp, still hoping that her farm training would soon lead to emigration to Palestine. But there was a strange twist of events.

The International League for Peace and Freedom [said] that they are going to take a certain amount of children between the ages of twelve and fifteen into Denmark to teach them farming. . . . The League [fought] against any persecution. . . . The Danish [branch of the League] contacted the undercover Zionistic organizations. . . . The Zionist movement submitted the list . . . and they contacted us . . . but there was a price to be paid for that. You know, you had to buy yourself . . . into Denmark or buy yourself out of Czechoslovakia. It was up to the parents of the children whether they could afford to pay for this expensive emigration. . . . Transports were also going from Germany. . . . There were three transports going in '39 to Denmark [with] close to a hundred [children]. . . . [My brother] was too young. I was just lucky. I fell into the age requirement.

Fortunately Hanna's parents were able to raise the necessary money and she left Czechoslovakia in October 1939 when she was fourteen.

You know, looking back, being that [age], for me it was a fantastic adventure, and looking back, I many, many times in my life thought, "How selfish was I." . . . It took me years before I could even think how my parents must have felt about that. It took me years before I even wanted to see pictures of my parents on the platform at the train.

Things were really getting bad, and we knew that they were not going to get any better. . . . We left after the war broke out. . . . I was on my own. I was just fourteen. . . . We sat on the train and we sang Hebrew songs . . . and going through Berlin, we were in this compartment all closed in. . . . I was in love with somebody and he was on the train. And then, you know, you got there and you broke down.

In Denmark, Hanna was separated from her companions and sent to a small farm where the family spoke only Danish. She was shocked by the severity of the Danish winter, the lack of electricity and running water, and her inexperience with farm life under such conditions. Hanna tried to telephone a friend from the transport, but this involved using a crank-handled telephone with a Danish operator placing the call and the attempt left her frustrated and isolated. Within this family of six

we could not communicate at all. . . . I cried many a tear and I didn't want to write home any letters. [I said] everything was fine when I wrote home because I know that they had more than their share . . . and they were happy that I was out of that situation. . . . Until April 1940 . . . the mail [from home] got through. . . . Most of the letters were censored. My brother . . . enclosed [his] cartoons in the mail. . . . As a matter of fact, my parents sent the farmer some presents for . . . Christmas. . . . It took me, I would say, a good thirty years before I even started to reread the letters. I just didn't want to.

She did not want to tell her family how harsh her life really was.

I had a completely unheated room, sort of outside . . . in the servants' quarters.
. . . My room was so cold that in the morning my sheets were frozen from my
breath. My blankets were frozen. . . . I did all the farm chores and pumped the
water in the evening so you could have water for cooking in the morning. . . .
If you pumped the water in the morning the pump was absolutely frozen. . . .
You start your fire in the morning in the kitchen but the water that was in the
kitchen was [also] frozen so you had to hack the ice. . . . We didn't have any
boots or anything like that so we always had to write to the League [for Peace
and Freedom] and ask for boots [and] they sort of collected clothing for us.
Once in awhile [a representative] came but we always used to make fun of her,
us kids, because she never did anything for us. She would take our name and
say, "I will send you a pair of boots," but she didn't. So we had these wooden
shoes and we stuck them with straw to keep them warm.

I think the farmer was pretty much disillusioned with me because I really did
not know anything. I did not know any farming and in the morning you had to
cook this oatmeal-porridge and in the beginning I did not know how to do that.
. . . [But] the Danes were very good-natured people so they just felt sorry and
they took us. Not only that, but we were a helping hand, and we didn't get paid.
. . . But I got along fine. . . . My first Christmas present from the farmer in 1939
was a silver spoon . . . [and] they got me an old dilapidated bike [because] you
cannot move around unless you can ride a bike. . . . I never knew how to ride a
bike . . . and I learned. In the winter we used to put rope around the tires instead
of snow tires. . . . The snow was very, very deep.

In April 1940, the Germans occupied Denmark.

I recall this quite vividly—suddenly, one morning, the whole German army
marching through the field into the farm—a cavalry on horses—and they settled
themselves down in the barn. . . . I just didn't want to get out of my room. The
farmer knew that I spoke German and he wanted me out there to communicate
with the soldiers. . . . I would not do that.

[The farmer knew I was Jewish] but I don't think that ever was a question.
. . . Before World War II . . . there was no Jewish Question [in Denmark]. . . .
For the farmer, [he just thought the situation] was very advantageous because
the Germans would pay a lot. . . . The Germans stayed on the farm, I think,
about one week and then they moved on. They supplied their horses [with] hay
and they supplied themselves with . . . sausages. . . . We slaughtered pigs at the
time, which I learned how to do and make sausages, which I learned how to do
. . . and then they moved on.

Hanna could not move from this farm because she was under a mandatory six-month contract. But by the late spring of 1940 she was able

to move closer to where many of her friends from the transport had settled. At least now she was not quite so isolated, and she could attend Zionist meetings once or twice a month—held despite the German occupation. On this farm, her chores were quite similar—kindling the fires, working in the fields, milking fourteen cows in one hour, caring for the chickens—while still sleeping in an unheated room where "the outside wall . . . was cracked so all the cold air was coming in." But here there was electricity and running water. She was also invited to eat her meals with the family. They even "made me a birthday party and they invited all [my friends]." This family was fortunate as well in having a washing machine.

[Although it] was run by hand, that was more than on the other farm. And I remember putting the clothes in the machine, boiling your water and bringing the water and putting it into the machine and turning the machine by hand and always I had fifteen turns. I was learning Hebrew and I [would say] fifteen Hebrew words.

At this time Hanna's understanding of the Danish attitude toward the German occupation was limited to feedback from the local farmers.

I did not know at that time about all the underground which was going around in Denmark. That I did not know until 1942. I did not know about the sabotages which were done in the big cities. That I did not know. I only lived in a little tiny rural [area] so it would be extremely unfair to say that all the Danes were pro-Germanic. All I know is just where I lived . . . I think they got a lot of money because . . . they were exporting [pork and bacon to] the Germans.

Hanna's social experience was also limited to the farm community.

I went to a couple of barn dances where the farm boys came, and I had no clothes because I started developing. I grew up very fast, and I used to run with safety pins all around because I had no clothes, no clothes at all.

In 1941, Hanna and her friends heard that they might have a chance to get to Palestine.

We got [word] that a transport is going to Palestine and [they] were transporting . . . thirty [at a time]. Because we couldn't go any other way because the war was going on, we were going to go to Sweden, to Finland, to Russia, and that way to Palestine. . . . We got our papers and a little luggage was sent. . . . One transport went, and they got stuck in the Finnish-Russian conflict. . . . Some . . .

had to come back. . . . Some of the children . . . got through. . . . One of my friends got through. . . . [Our] luggage went but we didn't go.

Hanna again wanted to move to a different place at the end of her six-month contract.

You see, I was very hungry—I think we all were—for some kind of education. At that time I spoke Danish and I wrote Danish. . . . If you live there you just pick it up. And I wanted to better myself, to go higher in life. . . . Of course, at that time girls couldn't get into agricultural schools. . . . Or maybe they could, but we never thought that it was our role to do that. It never occurred to us. It was not the way in Europe at all. . . . In Denmark, they had these finishing schools [where] girls from better families learned the proper way of housekeeping and entertainment. . . . They were like boarding schools. . . . So I started to write to different schools. . . . I tried to strike a bargain with them . . . that I would be a maid in the school or a maid to the mistress . . . of the school for free tuition. And one school . . . did reply.

I took my toothbrush and my knapsack and I took my bicycle and I biked for hours. . . . It was a terrible let-down because on the farm I was one of them. . . . At the school, I certainly was not one of them. All of the girls here were from good families and they were learning how to be mistresses of the houses . . . and I was a chamber maid . . . to the owner of the school and I got my tuition free that way. . . . I thought that everybody hated me, looked down on me. . . . I didn't see any of [my friends]. . . . I was isolated. I was the only one who was in [this] position—who didn't pay tuition, who didn't have textbooks—and I was very unhappy. I was extremely unhappy. I had no money at all, I mean, really, no money. And so I used to copy these textbooks and study at night [and] then I got up early in the morning to do the housework . . . and then go to classes.

I didn't sleep in the dorm. I slept in the maid's quarters. . . . [The other girls] went to dances together [with] a boy's military academy. . . . I couldn't. I was working and secondly I had no clothes. . . . I had the feeling that everybody was looking down on me.

But maybe I was wrong. That was the way I felt [but] when Christmas came they gave me a uniform because I only had one. . . . They gave me text books. . . . The girls got together and they gave me a ring. . . . They just knew that I was a strange bird. . . . I don't know [why I didn't tell them about myself]. Maybe I just wanted to be so much a part of them. . . . I was so tired. I was trying so hard to be part of them that I thought they didn't want part of me.

Hanna recalled that while copying textbooks into her own notebook ("I used to write everything in green ink"), she would leave her work under a window beneath the slanted dormer roof. She came back to her room one day to discover that the melting snow had leaked through and washed out all her carefully written work.

I thought it was the worst tragedy, but in the meantime my parents were somewhere in concentration camps. . . . I got a letter . . . that would be '42 . . . from my brother . . . when he said, "I thought I would be Bar Mitzvah but it doesn't look that way. That was the only thing I wanted to live for was for my Bar Mitzvah." . . . Then I got a letter from my parents also saying that this is the last letter. . . . They have been selected. . . . So, at that time, I tried to commit suicide.

A physician on staff at the school took a special interest in Hanna and encouraged her to look to the future, to plan for her life in Denmark until she was able to emigrate to Palestine. After Hanna finished her schooling, this doctor found her a job with the family of a banker. She was seventeen years old and had a clear sense of reality.

You knew if you had stayed [in Prague] you [might] not survive. . . . [In Denmark] . . . I knew that I had plenty of food to eat, which I did. I became real fat. I knew that I had a roof over my head. I spoke Danish. Nobody was on my back. The Germans were in Denmark for two years, but you really didn't feel them that much. I mean, I didn't. . . . One thing I never went through—this "finding myself." I didn't have that kind of problem. . . . You knew you were lucky. You knew that, you felt it, you smelled it.

Anti-German sentiment grew among the Danes and an underground movement swelled. They called themselves "Radishes" because the Danish national colors were red and white and the radish grew underground. When this group passed on the details of Nazi persecution in Europe, some of Hanna's friends from the transport feared that their luck was running out and that the Germans would move next against the Jewish population in Denmark.

In the summer of 1943, the underground circulated news that actions against the Jews in Denmark were imminent. They also made contacts with the group from the transport and arranged for a communication chain in case of such danger.

[But] the person who was supposed to contact me left to save his own skin without contacting me. . . . He went to the coast of Sweden. . . . [Then] one day a Dane came and picked me up . . . a young man from the underground. . . . He said, "We are going hiding." By that time things were already brewing. You knew. There was a lot of . . . sixth sense for these things. . . . I went to the coast

on a bike, and we went to a church and stayed in the church for one week. . . .
[We] slept under the pews [and] they brought some food. . . . I was the only
female and the only Jew . . . [other than a] mother and her daughter who [were
old] and pretty feeble. . . . Most of them were Danish officers who were there
at the time. . . . They were underground but they wanted to flee . . . to Sweden
. . . and there were [other] people who were in the Danish army that probably
had . . . anti-Nazi [feelings].

The plan was to use small boats to escape to Sweden—the neutral
refuge.

Every night we went to the beach to see if a boat came. And the thing was
this—the Danish fishermen . . . took you over but you had to pay, and I had
nothing. . . . So, the ones who could pay more . . . got in first, and the ones who
didn't pay anything . . . had to sneak themselves [aboard]. . . . So I got on a . . .
fishing boat, a herring boat, a little tiny boat, and there were twenty-five of us.
We go into the hull of the ship and they cover us up with straw . . . and we
are sailing and sailing and sailing. . . . Well . . . the distance is really nothing,
and we were on the boat for ten hours and we are getting nowhere. . . . And we
were right on the open sea and this is October now and . . . the Germans always
raid right after the Jewish holiday. It was right after Yom Kippur and suddenly
. . . [we] find out that this fisherman . . . did not have a map. He didn't have a
compass. . . . He just sailed according to the stars. . . . We wound up [on] the
Polish side of the Kattegat and the Germans came on board the ship—the German
soldiers with their bayonets. . . . There was herring on top of the tarpaulin and
we were under the herrings . . . and they were walking on top of the boat, and,
you know, your heart was in your throat, to say the least. . . . To this day, I
think that the Germans must have known that we were there. It was impossible
that they did not know when they examined this little shanty . . . that we were
there. . . . And [they] ordered the fisherman to go back to Denmark which we
did. We turned around on the same boat and went in the other direction. Well,
by that time everybody was getting seasick. Everybody was, but I didn't because
I hadn't eaten for four days and had nothing to throw up.
We got to Sweden eventually. . . . It was twenty-two hours later. . . . Much
later we found out that . . . the fisherman . . . was really a criminal and his license
was revoked, his compass was revoked, and he was trying to make money. Then
somebody told me later on that he really was not a fisherman at all.
Suddenly . . . you see the coast. . . . We didn't know if it was the Danish coast,
the Swedish coast, the Polish coast, and suddenly we see all of these little
rowboats coming out to us, rowing out to us and waving and it really was
something. . . . And the Swedes came over in the rowboats and they took us in.
. . . Now, we didn't even know where we landed, what town, and we all just
cried and laughed, and it was like seeing the Promised Land.

We set our foot on the land. It's a fishing village. And here's the boat full of twenty-five . . . people and . . . this fishing village . . . has never seen anything like that and they are starting to fight among each other. Now, Danish and Swedish is very similar, the language. When they get mad you can understand what they are talking about, and these fishing wives were fighting about who is going to go to whose house to eat because they set out big spreads for us.

[Later] the police came. They took our data and they took our fingerprints and they took our pictures and they took us to a high school. And there were more papers and more formalities and so on, and they assigned us to go to different places. Now in the meantime I was thinking, "Where are all [my friends from the transport]? Where did they go? . . . How am I going to get in touch with them?"

[The Swedish Red Cross] brought us clothes because there was nothing. I got my first pair of black panties, my first black bra, a black dress, and black stockings. . . . I was eighteen but I was as innocent as a baby. It was like [I was from] the last century. . . . [And then] they gave us birth control pills . . . and a douche. . . . I became so insulted, you have no idea.

[We were in] an agricultural boarding school. But they were on . . . a potato vacation break where kids go home and pick potatoes and then come back to school. The school had to start pretty soon so they had to empty the gym where we were sleeping. . . . What am I going to do? I had no idea where the other people were. . . . At that time I was eighteen. I was no more a child.

Again, relying on her own resources, Hanna got a job in the school's kitchen cleaning herring—a staple of the Swedish diet—for the next six months, until she found a nursing school which accepted her under the same financial arrangement she had arranged in Denmark, tuition in exchange for work.

The Swedish Red Cross paid for her train fare to the school in northern Sweden and gave her a small stipend. But Hanna could not afford a new uniform and again washed her used uniform at night and ironed it in the morning. She also attempted to learn Swedish quickly so that she could keep up with her courses. When the school told her they would only accept her services in exchange for tuition for one term, she was transferred to another nursing school closer to Stockholm with the same work-study agreement until she earned her certificate. By the end of the war, she was able to get a paying job in a mental hospital.

They stuck me right away into the very, very violent ward. . . . But I got paid. . . . So, I worked there and I celebrated my twentieth birthday there . . . and I started thinking about myself [as a] little more than a machine who works and thinking about myself being a young woman . . . with needs [and] having some kind of relationship, . . . what's going to be as far as my femininity was concerned.

A rumor started to circulate that those who escaped to Sweden from Denmark could now return to Denmark and become a Danish citizen. For Hanna, this was her chance to rid herself of her stateless identification, to achieve some security that was open only to Europeans with the "right papers." When she returned to Denmark, however, she was told the rumor was false. She could not get Danish citizenship. So, Hanna decided to return to Prague in 1946. There she learned that only an uncle, aunt, and a cousin who had been hidden in a convent had survived from her family.

I found some friends. I lived with my aunt and . . . I was trying to find some contact about the surviving people. I was running to Theresienstadt [the camp where her family perished]. I took the train and the bus to Theresienstadt. I wanted to get some kind of death certificate . . . to present to the American embassy [saying] "they are not alive" and thus the affidavit [which her parents had applied for] would come to me. . . . [I] got all those death certificates.

[Except] for my aunt who was there, and my uncle who was there, I felt nothing. I didn't feel I belonged. I just didn't feel. I didn't. I went to the house that we lived in, I went to the school. I went. I went to the *shul*.[2] I felt that it's not me, that's not for me. That's not my life. But I don't know where my life is. . . . I know this is not it because I feel worse being a stranger here . . . at home . . . than being a stranger in a strange land.

Hanna, however, completed her university studies in Czechoslovakia and then left the country after the Communist takeover. "Everybody was like under the Nazis. Everybody was afraid. . . . The smell of fear was worse than anything else." After another stay in Denmark and Sweden, her affidavit came through in 1950 and she started life again in the United States.

From the testimony of Hanna Seckel-Drucker

[2]Synagogue.

8 *Samuel*

The Germans invaded Samuel's home in Lithuania when he was nine-years-old and sent him to a labor camp with the men of his village. As an eleven-year-old, Samuel was deported to Auschwitz and was one of the very few children to survive the death camp. By his early teens, Samuel knew firsthand the brutality of the German advance troops and the sadism of the camp guards. Only luck, he believed, saved him.

The German troops advancing into the Soviet Union sought out anti-Semitic segments of the native population to help target, round up, and destroy the Jewish population. Tapping into native hostility against the Jews, the Germans instigated local pogroms and mass executions. Those areas where the native population aided the Germans had the highest death toll of Jewish population. It is estimated that ninety percent of the Jewish population of the Baltic countries, including Lithuania, perished during the war.

Samuel was born in 1932 in a small town in Lithuania in a community of about four hundred Orthodox Jews. His father and grandfather were flax merchants, providing a secure living for the family, and his mother had taught mathematics at the University of Riga before her marriage. As was customary in Schweksna, Samuel started *cheder* or religious school before he was five, staying from morning to night, and from the age of six attended public school until noon and then *cheder*. The inter-war period was a relatively calm one in Lithuania for the Jews since the newly formed Lithuanian government did not sanction discrimination or pogroms. Social anti-Semitism, however, persisted. When the war started, Samuel and his family initially felt relief that the Soviet Union had signed a non-aggression pact with Germany and felt somewhat protected by the Soviet occupation.

We knew that [the German Jews] were suffering, but we did not know that this could happen to us because in 1940 [when] the Russians came in, we thought Russia was a giant.

The reality of the Soviet occupation, however, was different. The Communist Party took over their home, moving the family into one area of the house, and his father, along with other well-to-do citizens, lost his business and became an employee of the Soviet government. In some cases, these Jewish businessmen worked for the same companies they had previously owned under the direction of a Lithuanian overseer who had joined the Communist movement. The children now attended Soviet schools and were subject to political indoctrination, including selective membership in Communist youth organizations.

It wasn't easy to get in. You had to bring up the fact that you were from the proletariat . . . [and if you weren't], like my dad, they sent you to Siberia. . . . [But] they didn't get to my father.

On June 22, 1941, the problems with the Soviet occupation ended and the German invasion began.

June the twenty-second on Sunday morning around three o'clock, [since] we lived only five miles away from the border, we heard the shelling upon our town and constantly. My father gathered all of us together and we didn't know where to go so we ran in the fields. . . . We knew if we were caught by the Germans it's not going to be good. . . . We didn't have any warning. In fact, the night before there [were many] celebrations . . . because that was the [first anniversary of the day] the Russians came into Lithuania. . . . We felt pretty secure. We thought that the Russians will defend . . . and conquer Germany with no pain. [But] when we went to the fields we saw a lot of Russians with their rifles going back. Some of them were without an arm already, bandaged, you know, with the horses running by themselves.
A couple of hours later we saw Germans already in our town, and we were surrounded everywhere, and we couldn't go back—neither here nor there. They were faster. . . . Where could you run?
The [pro-German] Lithuanians had white [arm] bands. . . . They were trying to take revenge because . . . a few Jewish people that were in the Communist

Party . . . used to confiscate [their] grain . . . not because they wanted it [but] because it was a government order. . . . [These Lithuanians] stuffed them with grain down the throat and they suffocated. . . . And they shot a few girls that worked in the . . . Russian command post . . . only secretaries, you know, but still they took revenge.

The Germans ordered all the Jews to move into the Jewish quarter of the town, cramping six families into single homes.

The SS came with the Lithuanians and . . . the Lithuanians pointed out where all the Jews lived and where there were Jewish homes. And they took . . . the men to the synagogue. When they came into my house . . . I laid down on the couch. I didn't want to see them. I was afraid so I covered myself. . . . When the SS came in they asked my mother, "Who is sleeping here?" and she said, "That's my little boy," and [they said] to my mother, "Let him come along with us," and they took me . . . or else I would have stayed there with everybody else in that home town. Three months later . . . they were all shot.

When I came . . . to the synagogue . . . I saw my father, the rabbi . . . young men, strong people . . . old people, and a few young like me. . . . They had a doctor from the town and he was a good man . . . a Lithuanian. He had to examine every one of us . . . and upstairs [in] the women's part where women used to . . . pray . . . there was a barber . . . an anti-Semite. . . . He made a cross this way and this way in our hair, so they called it a *lausenstrasse*—a lice promenade. . . . Then we got beatings from . . . an SS guy with a whip.

That was Friday night. The rabbi's beard was cut and . . . they told . . . another Jew . . . to hold the rabbi's hair in his hands and this man had to put a torch to his hair and burn it. . . . Our Torahs . . . the prayerbooks . . . the *talesim*,[1] everything was on the ground and they told us to tramp on it. . . . For a couple of hours [we had to do] all kinds of calisthenics . . . with your arms and crawling on the ground and jumping each time if you didn't do it the way they told you, they tortured [you]. They threw dollars, American dollars, and rubles on the ground to see if someone . . . would pick it up . . . purposely as a temptation. Can you imagine their sadistic minds?

Saturday morning . . . they told . . . women to come and bring us food. So the women came and brought us food. They didn't know what is going to happen to us. . . . They thought they would be able to see us and they approached the gate. . . . The SS started to shoot over their heads so they thought they were going to be shot and they ran away. . . . One of these . . . Lithuanians [who] is now in Chicago . . . brought it up for me—a package from my mother. Some food. . . . He tried . . . but they took it away afterwards anyway. . . . He was like the others. He went from town to town and house to house pointing out the Jews

[1]Jewish prayershawls.

[but] he knew me because I played with him. In fact I [once] saved his life in the big pond. We were going skating and he fell in and I held onto him until his uncle came. . . . If not, he would have been dead.

Samuel, his father, and the others were loaded onto trucks and taken to a labor camp near Heidekrug, Germany, where they were put into work units digging ditches, leveling ground, working in gravel pits. Samuel's father, still a strong, robust man, headed one of these units. There were a few other boys slightly older than Samuel, but Samuel was singled out.

The guard . . . made me clean his apartment, clean his shoes, bring food to the [other] guards . . . peel potatoes [and other light work]. . . . I really don't know why. It was a chance. To this day, I don't even know. Maybe [the Almighty] had a purpose.

[Because] I cleaned . . . sometimes I used to get leftovers, you know, what he used to throw out, and I used to take it. He didn't see those things. . . . I used to give them to my father and my uncle. . . . That was from '41 until '43.

Every month they selected . . . and they used to ask, "Who wants to go home?" But, of course, there was no home. They were actually being shot. . . . My father wanted to go home so they put his name down. . . . I [told] the guard [whose shoes I cleaned] that I would like to go with him if I could. He said, "No. You we need yet. You cannot go," and I said, "Since you won't let me go, can my father stay?" So he let him stay. . . . Because I had contact with [this guard], I could talk to him. Usually you cannot talk to them.

Within three months of his arrival, Samuel learned the fate of the rest of his family.

We learned that all the women and children [were ordered by the Germans] to gather together and bring their jewelry and possessions, whatever clothes [they had]. [They were told] they were going to see the men—us, that were taken to work. They put them all in trucks. The Lithuanians drove the trucks and the SS were there and they took them from our town six kilometers out in the woods. There were already the ditches dug and the SS troopers, the Germans, and the Lithuanians were already drunk. They had machine guns all ready. They told them to undress in front of the graves, they took . . . all the possessions . . . away, and they machine-gunned everyone of them to death. Some of them were even alive and they buried them alive. The blood came through the ground the next morning.

[Later on] we saw clothes that came from our homes, clothes that people wore when they were taken . . . so we knew what happened to them.

Only nine-years-old when he arrived, Samuel was the youngest in the work camp. He remained fortunate in his work detail, doing errands for the guards instead of constant hard labor, but he was still under threat of punishment.

Once I went . . . to bring the food for the guards from the SS kitchen . . . and the guards let me go alone. . . . There was one house [on the way] where the woman was very sympathetic and she used to give me bread . . . a German . . . an older person. There were quite a few of them who were very good but they could do nothing. . . . One day it was raining and for some reason the guards [were watching me bring back the food]. I turned around because I had some bread [from the German woman] on me. . . . The guards started to shoot at me. . . . When I came back, the guard told the *lager führer*[2] of the camp what I had done [the same man I had worked for]. They lined up all the Jews . . . and he gave me ten beatings with . . . his whip and my father had to see this. . . . I collapsed on the floor. . . . He says, "That will happen to everyone of you if you are going to do something like this." . . . You know it is very difficult to figure them out. It was very difficult. Here I am cleaning his room and shining his shoes and when it came [time] for me to get a beating, he beat me good. He didn't give me one or two, he gave me ten for having a piece of bread.

You know what they used to do in the Heidekrug camp? In the middle of the night the SA and the SS used to come in and they used to make us [jump] from our bunks and [do] all kinds of calisthenics—sports they called it. . . . They used to bang with the butts [of their rifles], you know, into the doors, and when we heard them, we [knew] right away.

In the middle of 1943, orders came to evacuate the Jews from the camps in this area.

Now we didn't know what was going on, but we knew that it was no good. We thought we're going to be shot. Finally Dr. S. came along and he said, "Since you are good workers, you are going to a very good place. You will really enjoy being there. You'll be all together. I'm giving you a good recommendation that you are . . . the best workers that I had."

Five hundred people traveled about eight days in cattle trains to arrive at Auschwitz-Birkenau. Samuel was eleven-years-old.

There was a selection—left, right, left, right—and my uncle . . . went to the left. My father was to the right. They sent me also to the left which was [to]

[2]Commandant.

the truck and I thought the truck would be much better. But I wanted to be with my father and I saw my father on the other side. In that back and forth, back and forth, I jumped down [from] that truck and I went back to the group that [still] had to be selected. And this time, an SS man pointed me to the right . . .

and I was right next to my father and we went into the camp. I thought walking would be more difficult than on the truck, but as it turned out, it was better.

When we came into the camp, we saw women with violins, and I remember distinctly the march even today in my ears. I thought this was heaven.

They gave us right away a number and told us to go into the delousing place and when we went in there we saw . . . these showers and everything else. It could have been a different shower, too, you know. Thank God. But this was . . . real. . . . They gave us cold water and then they disinfected us and then they gave us the striped clothes—the first time we had striped clothes—and then we went in a quarantine. . . . I was told that there was a separate bunk for children . . . but I don't know because I didn't see it myself. . . . I stayed with my father.

Our commando built tracks so instead of [having a] selection, [the transports could go] right into the gas chamber. We saw every day [transports] coming from Greece. I will never forget as long as I am going to live. There was this one transport that came in from Salonika and everybody was dead and there was a convoy of . . . twenty-five to thirty trucks at least. There was one girl alive. She was sitting on the top of a . . . pile of corpses from the transport. . . . It stands out in my eyes, you know, her face. And she also went into the gas chamber.

Every Sunday there were selections. I remember Dr. Mengele coming up to me once. He used to go with a lot of officers . . . and when I stood up and I made myself like this—tall, you know—he says to me in German, . . . "You don't have to make yourself big. I see what you are." But he passed [me] by. . . . But they asked me how old I am and I said that I am fifteen. I lied about my age because, you see, when you are in camp . . . you are undernourished [and you look younger]. You could get away with a lie. . . . When you are in such a situation as a child somehow your brain works differently. . . . You [also] remember vividly. You remember details.

What [the guards did] for recreation [was to make us] take our jackets upside down, put our arms through this way and button up in the back. They used to load us up with stones and we used to carry [them] from the camp to the outside of the camp for about ten to fifteen yards and then back for three to four hours every Sunday.

They taught us how to put our heads up and our heads down, how to approach an officer, which was with the right gestures. Otherwise, you know, if you didn't do it the right way, right away you got slapped. We saw all kinds of tortures and beatings in the barracks. They used to make us jump in the middle of the night . . . up and down and up and down and the boards [from the bunks] used to fall on [our] noses. . . . In the morning . . . the Lithuanians and Ukrainians [guards] . . . used to call the prisoners to the wire, to the gate. When the German

calls you, you come . . . but you had the right not to [with these other guards].
. . . If you did go, they had the right to shoot you and that's what they did. . . .
You used to see hundreds and hundreds every morning lying flat on the ground,
dead. . . . [The old prisoners] told us, "Don't do it. Don't go." . . . [But] you
come fresh, you know. . . . [You're not sure] when to respond and when not to
respond.

There wasn't a day that I didn't suffer from hunger and . . . hunger pain is so
severe. . . . They used to give us cigarette rations . . . cigarettes, no food. They
used to give us three or four cigarettes a week. I used to sell . . . those cigarettes
for bread. There were people that did not care about food. They didn't care if
they lived or died or what happened to them. They wanted that smoke and
cigarettes . . . and they went fast.

In the cold . . . they made us get up at four o'clock in the morning. They made
us stand in line to drink up that coffee . . . then right in line for three hours. . . .
It varied. And God forbid, if somebody was missing, you'd stay until they found
him . . . dead or . . . alive.

They made us write letters back home. Maybe they want to find out if somebody is alive yet. . . . I wrote to my cousin in Kovno [and] my cousin received
the letter. . . . We knew that they are going to censor it every line we write, [so
we wrote] that we are fine, we are working, we are all together and everything
is nice, the food is very good, and we enjoy being where we are.

Late in 1943, volunteers were demanded for another camp, and Samuel
and his father, figuring that it could not be worse than Auschwitz, signed
up. Five thousand of them traveled by cattle car to Warsaw, where they
were put to work cleaning up the rubble of the destroyed ghetto. They
also built barracks and crematoria.

There was hell there. [People] died from typhus, spotted typhus, black fever.
One morning, I contacted that too. . . . They took me away to the . . . so-called
hospital . . . for four weeks. . . . There were no sanitary conditions. . . . The straw
sacks where we were sleeping were infested. . . . I don't know what happened
to me because I do not remember a thing in those four weeks.

Returned to the barracks after a month, Samuel was helped by a French
Jew in charge of the barracks who sent him to work in the prison kitchen.
For those few months he could get extra soup and give some to his father
as well.

There was a selection in Warsaw and I . . . asked if something could be done.
. . . My father shouldn't have to go. . . . [Somehow my father] was hidden where

all the foods are hidden . . . until the selection was over. [This man] figured that since I was a child, little, you know, that I needed somebody.

As the Soviet army approached Warsaw in the summer of 1944, most of the camp was evacuated, leaving about two hundred people behind. About five thousand prisoners walked from Warsaw to Kutno on the way to Lodz. Walking from dawn to dark, the prisoners tried to dig into the ground to get water when they finally stopped to rest.

Would you believe we got water? We dug and we got water. One place we marched . . . there was a big, big river, and they said, "You can go and drink that water," and everybody jumped right in. . . . It was so hot. . . . And they started to machine gun, to shoot, and everybody ran right out.

From Warsaw to Kutno by foot, to Dachau by train, Samuel estimates that one-half of their original group perished. His final destination was Muhldorf where they built a repair depot for the Luftwaffe. Under the supervision of German civilians, they worked double shifts, carrying cement on their backs. In late April 1945, the inmates were informed that they were to be taken to the Alps and exchanged for German troops.

We were traveling for a couple of days and all of a sudden the doors were opened up and they told us we were in Pocking in Bavaria . . . very close to the Alps . . . and they said, "You can go." So everybody was happy and everybody was trying to jump and dance and kiss whoever survived and then all of a sudden [we saw] the Germans coming, the Luftwaffe. . . . They surrounded us and they said, "You Jews, you escaped," and they put us all in a big field and they had machine guns . . . and they were ready to kill us. . . . My father said to me, "Come, son, give me your hand and if we will die we will die together," and I gave him my hand. . . . Then the *bürgermeister*[3] from that town came and he said, "The Jews did not escape. They were told that they can leave." . . . They listened and they did not kill us. They gathered us together again. They put us back into the trains and again started to go back and forth, back and forth. . . . The Germans already had their machine guns on top. The Americans with their planes saw a transport with the machine guns on top. They thought it was German Army— Wehrmacht—and they started to shoot up the train. . . . The SS guards . . . opened up the doors again so we [could] go underneath [the train] and a lot of them got killed that way by the Americans because these planes came down low over our heads and the bullets strayed.

[The Germans] gathered us back again . . . and we knew that something wasn't

[3]Mayor or political head of a community.

right. We thought that maybe they would take us into the right place to let us out and then that would be the end. I mean they would shoot us.

Finally, on April 28, they came to a town called Seeshaupt.

The doors were opened up. We were afraid to go because we thought maybe it was another trick, and we saw a different kind of army and then we saw it was the U.S.A. We started to jump and then the Americans came over to us and they said, "Don't worry about it. You are free and you can do whatever you want." They gave us rations and they gave us food and people started to drink . . . evaporated milk, cans of milk, and a lot of them died. A lot of my friends. . . . I drank too, but I figured all right, I am free, I'll eat a little at a time because I didn't want to stuff myself. [At the same time] I thought, I'm still in camp. I'm going to put away a little for later.

After he and his father were liberated, Samuel started to work with the American army, still concealing that he was only fifteen-years-old.

We used to confiscate cars from the Germans, from the Nazis, and give [them] to the military personnel. . . . In Dachau we had the SS troops there, prisoners. We used to get them to fix cars. . . . I used to wear a uniform with a gun and everything. . . . I didn't take vengeance, but I should have.

Samuel feels that he must stand witness to what he experienced:

[As] witnesses to these murderous acts and to the genocide, we must remember and tell our generation and our children and our children's children for generations to come, that such a massacre of Jewish people should never come again, and not only to the Jewish people, but this could happen to anybody. Therefore we must tell [our] children that they should be on guard constantly against dictatorship. . . . [So many died], so many innocent women, children, old men, learned men, rabbis, professors, so many people that gave so much to humanity. . . .

From the testimony of Samuel Sherron

9   *Myer*

Myer recaptures the images and dreams of his childhood in an Orthodox shtetl in eastern Poland, from the joys of making his own toys to the nightmares of anti-Semitic attacks. He describes his evolution from the seclusion of the Hasidic yeshiva into the secular world with the advent of Hitler and the harsh realities of his deportation to Siberia. With vivid detail he recalls the Soviet social and economic system and the adaptive techniques which ensured his survival.

The Nazi-Soviet Pact of 1939 awarded eastern Poland to the Soviets in exchange for their agreement not to challenge Germany's invasion of western Poland. The Soviet government then pressured the foreign nationals under their control to accept Soviet citizenship. Those who refused, like Myer and his family, were deported to Siberia. Over a quarter of a million Polish Jews were deported to work camps where many died from disease, hunger, and harsh working conditions. Those who agreed to accept Soviet citizenship could remain in Soviet-controlled eastern Poland. However, Germany's invasion of the Soviet Union in June 1941 brought this territory and its people back under Nazi control and persecution.

When Myer was born in 1914 at the start of World War I, he and his family were evacuated from their home in Rudnik, Poland, a small town in Galicia. Only five kilometers from the Russian border, their home town had become part of the battlefront. They spent the four war years in Czechoslovakia while his father fought in the Polish army. When they returned home in 1918, much had changed for the family: injuries and trauma from the war had taken their toll on Myer's father and he died when Myer was seven, leaving him with a few precious memories:

I remember a couple of incidents with my father, only when I walked with him to the *shul* back and forward. But one thing I will never forget—I guess because I keep reminding myself—when I was three years old . . . he carried me to the *cheder*[1]. . . . You see at home if a boy was three years old, the father carried him . . . the first time. . . . I will never forget it.

Before his death, Myer's father had salvaged what remained of their small house in Rudnik and built a room—a room that housed the family with its five children as well as serving as a small grocery store.

Rudnik, a town of about ten thousand, had about two hundred Jewish families before World War II. There were many limitations on Jewish occupations, including restrictions against owning land. Many in the town, like Myer's father, were shopkeepers. The community functioned under the centuries' old concept of *kehilla*—a network of fellowship organizations or *chevrot* which provided services for all of the Jews. Myer's father served in the *chevra lena* which took turns sitting up at night with the sick so that the family could rest. He had also been a member of the *chevra kadisha* which prepared the dead for burial, and Myer's mother did the same for the women of the community. But when Myer's father died, his family was proud that it did not have to depend on the *kehilla* for financial support because one of Myer's brothers, already in the United States, sent money regularly.

Without him . . . we would have been forced to receive from the *tsedukah*[2] and on account of him, we were a respectable family. We even gave *tsedukah*. You know something? I found out later when I came to . . . this country that when he sent money, he borrowed the money. . . . He paid interest for the money that he sent us.

Myer's family lived in a Jewish section, but there was a church on their street and their customers were both Jewish and Christian. As far as other children were concerned,

you couldn't play with them. You went to school with them . . . [but] we were dressed differently. . . . We had the *payes*[3] and I was always the target. They

---

[1]Jewish elementary school.
[2]Charity.
[3]Earlocks worn by traditional Jewish males.

pulled me by the *payes*. . . . It was a little difficult because when I started public school I didn't know a word of Polish . . . [only] Yiddish. . . . You see . . . the barrier was there. Maybe if I would have known Polish, I would have been able to communicate with them. . . . The teachers . . . were very nice. . . . I don't think they discriminated. They didn't like the way we dressed or, I guess, they would have enjoyed if they could talk to me right away in Polish, but it didn't take a long time. I learned . . . from the kids.

I lived on the street with the church. When they went to the church I could play on the street, but when they went home from church, we had to lock the door. . . . There was something in the ceremony . . . that the Jew is a Christ-killer and they have to beat them up. . . . [So] we locked ourselves in and [pulled] the shutters closed when the church was letting out.

Some dreams still follow me now, that I get beaten up. You know, the worst dream is—and I had it so many times—that I just cannot run. Here they let out from the church . . . and the power is just not in me to run. . . . The worst thing was on Easter. They make . . . [an image of] a Jew . . . with a beard and they dropped him and everybody beat him and . . . they hung him up on a pole. . . . That was going on in the town square.

In 1959 . . . on Succos[4] I was there in Borough Park [with my] nephew. . . . [I was sleeping] on the second floor and my window was right near . . . a corner . . . with a telephone pole or an electric pole, and I woke up in the morning and I see a dummy hanging. I start screaming and the whole picture got back to me from my home town. And later, slowly . . . I calmed down and I realized what that is. That was the . . . first couple years when the Dodgers moved out from Brooklyn, and the Brooklyn people were trying to adopt the Yankees as their team . . . but they lost the World Series . . . so . . . I saw a Yankee [hanging]. . . . You know that it's a funny thing. A good thing, you forget. . . . Bad things you try to forget [but] you cannot.

Myer's father had been a religious man who believed in the importance of a secular education as well. After his death, Myer's sister and her Hasidic[5] husband moved in with the family and the atmosphere of the home changed to strict observance. As a result, Myer was taken out of public school at the age of fourteen and sent to a Hasidic yeshiva.[6]

First I went to a small town . . . Krychow . . . [near] Lublin. . . . The rabbi they named after the city, the rabbi from Krychow. . . . I was sleeping in the *bes hamidrash*, in the synagogue . . . and they sent me food from home and the

[4]Jewish harvest festival.

[5]Pertaining to Hasidism, a religious movement founded in Eastern Europe in the eighteenth century which emphasizes emotional devotion to God.

[6]Jewish academy of advanced religious studies.

rabbi's maid cooked it for me. . . . I was to do nothing but to study. . . . Everybody studies, but very few actually became rabbis. [It was] my mother's dream, and I guess every mother's dream. If that had been my goal, I would have been a rabbi, I guess.

I liked artwork . . . but that was an impossible dream. . . . I was always good in art in school. I always got an "A" and I liked to work with wood because that was the main thing I had a chance to do. You know, everything came packed in crates and the wood was tempting. You can do something with this, so I always built something and that's how I start [to make] a grogger[7] . . . I made myself a grogger every year for Purim.[8] [Now the groggers I make are] in the Jewish Museum [in Philadelphia] and the New York [Jewish] Museum.

At home, if you wanted a toy you had to build it. I even made myself a football. . . . Who could afford to buy a football? . . . We went to the slaughter-house, and there are certain things in the animal . . . like a bag . . . like the inner tube of the football. . . . It didn't last long, but the guys in the slaughterhouse . . . saved this for us, and we filled this up with air and we made a cover from old shoes.

[In the yeshiva] it wasn't a conflict . . . and when [they] needed some artwork they always called me. . . . Usually they made signs for collecting money on the street . . . so they always called me. . . . I remember the Radomsker rabbi came to Cracow . . . and he wasn't a very well man . . . and they didn't let . . . in any people only . . . the big shots. . . . [So] they gave me paper to make a sign . . . "Welcome Rabbi" and of course I made the sign and I got to stay there and I was thinking that that was the biggest reward, the biggest pay, I ever got.

For the next seven years, Myer studied at various yeshivot. He was unaware of the events in Germany in the early 1930s because the yeshiva students were forbidden to read any secular material including newspapers. Myer dates his curiosity and concern for events outside the yeshiva from the time he was twenty-one. It was 1935.

I don't know. I just started. . . . You become aware that there is a world going on . . . that this is not the whole world. If the world would depend on us, there would be no world. . . . You know according to the studies, the world is flat . . . because it says clearly in the *Gemorah*[9] that the world has four corners and in every corner stays an angel . . . that [together] hold the world on their shoulders and if I will not be so religious and good, if I would stop studying, then one of the angels can slip his shoulder and the whole world can collapse. And when I started reading articles . . . about the galaxy, . . . it was a new world for me. I

[7]Noisemaker.
[8]Jewish holiday in early spring commemorating survival in ancient Persia.
[9]Part of the Talmud, involving traditional rabbinic commentary.

was trying to find out more and . . . I enrolled in the library. . . . There were a lot of private libraries. . . . There was a very nice man and he recommended . . . books and later I got myself a job.

I quit the yeshiva. . . . I was thinking that [my mother] will never forgive me. For her it was a shock. . . . I explained it to her and I told her that I would be religious but, you know, you couldn't talk much with Mother. . . . She was never so fanatically religious. . . . It was only since Father died and [my] brother-in-law moved in.

The first thing that I did is to get a secular education . . . seventh grade privately in the first year and [then] I started business college. When I finished business college, I got a job as a bookkeeper. . . . I lived in Cracow . . . and I took advantage of every lecture I could.

I cut . . . the *payes* systematically, every week a little bit . . . a little shorter. . . . I didn't have the guts to do it [all at once].

By the time the war started, all of Myer's brothers had left Poland, eventually settling in the United States or Palestine.

I was the only one left at home. . . . Maybe I would have a chance [to leave] but I didn't try because I didn't want to do it to Mother.

The Germans bombed Cracow on the first day of the invasion in September 1939 and as soon as Myer could leave the bomb shelter, he made his way back to his mother in Rudnik, only to find the town in complete chaos—the Polish authorities had fled and the anti-Semitic feelings of many Poles resulted in the beating and robbing of the Jewish population. When the German troops arrived,

they didn't open the doors. They knocked the doors open and . . . they took all the men out into the market square . . . [both] Jews and non-Jews. . . . After they rounded up, they say, "Who is not a Jew shall leave. . . . Anything you want from the Jews, take." . . . In the meantime . . . most of the town . . . is on fire. . . . They shot a couple of people just if they didn't like them. . . . They shot . . . a guy . . . because he didn't give [them his] watch. . . . Oh, how they beat. . . . If somebody wore a beard, they cut off only one half, they didn't cut off the whole. And they took pictures. It was a miserable thing to watch, to be [there]. . . . And me, they cut the hair here in the middle with a machine . . . all the way back. . . . I had very nice hair, wavy hair.

It was like around twelve or one o'clock at night, and they came in with a tank and they say to line up and they will shoot us. The tank will kill us. . . . And do you know something? It didn't matter to me. It didn't matter a bit if they killed me or not. . . . I didn't care. . . . The chances of survival were very little anyhow. If he doesn't kill me now, he kills me later. I can suffer more. That's all. I didn't know if my family is still alive. . . . So who needs to be alive?

In the meantime they took pictures. . . . I could not understand how they can watch it. . . . It was like to them a show, you know. . . . Somehow, in the last minute, a guy comes, an officer . . . and gave orders to let us go. They gave the orders that in five minutes if they find somebody in the street, they will kill him. So I run . . . and I was trying . . . to find shelter . . . and another man comes . . . and he didn't recognize me, and I didn't recognize him. His beard was half cut off and half the hair. . . . [It was] my brother-in-law . . . and we start crying.

Gathering the family together, Myer and his brother-in-law fled with them to the woods for a few days, dodging sprays of bullets from planes overhead. After the invasion, the Germans rounded up survivors from the woods and returned them to Rudnik for labor units. But within two weeks the orders changed. The Germans pushed them five miles east, over the River San into Soviet territory.

They wanted to get rid of the Jews. It was very simple. Let the Russians have us. . . . They gave us twenty-four hours, but the [Poles] didn't give us any time. [As soon as] the order came out, they just chased us out because everybody just wanted to get . . . your property. . . . We formed our own militia . . . to keep order [and] so we wouldn't get slaughtered.

They arrived in a small town on the border along with refugees from several other villages evacuated by the Germans.

[It was] a little town and all of a sudden, it finds itself with four times the population. . . . Every Jew, every native there . . . took us in and gave us a room. . . . You know, it's a funny thing—to be a Jew is a big advantage because anywhere you come there are Jews. . . . *Gemillah chesed*. It means to do a favor. . . . We were not alone.

Forced to move further east as the Germans kept advancing, Myer and his family were met over and over again by welcoming Jewish communities.

Every Jewish family took in as many as they could. That doesn't mean as many as they had spare rooms [but] even if they had [some floor space]. And, of course, the synagogues were all packed with people, because the first thing that you do is you go to the synagogue. I thought of this many times when I came here and I see these plush carpets. . . . I think if our synagogues [then] had plush carpeting it would have been so much easier!

By late fall of 1939, the family settled in Grodek, near Lvov and under Soviet control. Again they found shelter with a host family, but Myer could not find work. Instead he supported the family by black-marketing—his introduction to the Soviet lifestyle.

Right away when the Russians came around, it became a black market. You couldn't get things. . . . They controlled it. . . . All that I had to do was stay in line and get something and later sell it on the black market because . . . you couldn't get . . . work.

In 1940, the Soviet authorities pressured them to accept Soviet citizenship and to emigrate to the Donbass coal region further east.

In the summer, around June [1940], they started catching every young man that they saw, and when they caught him, they checked him [to see] where he was born. If he was from the other side [western Poland] . . . they took and arrested him and sent [him] to Donbass . . . [and] if you go you become a Russian citizen. . . . In our group there was about eight or nine people. It varied. Some of them went back and we connected with other groups. [We were] mainly young men. Young and single. . . . I wouldn't call it a partisan group because a partisan group fights. . . . I was resisting and there were a lot of other young people that resisted. . . . We were just trying to be safe, just to hide and not get caught, and not be sent to Donbass.

My sister's daughter at that time was about eleven years old. . . . You see a child like this they didn't [check]. She was the go-between. . . . She helped us out. . . . On a Friday night, my sister's little girl came and she contacted us and she said they loaded the whole town on boxcars to ship them out and they don't know where. She sneaked away from the boxcar. . . . I was thinking they were taking my mother I don't know where. I went and voluntarily gave myself up, and that's how they shipped us to Siberia.

Thirty-five people, Jews and non-Jews, were packed into each boxcar designated to hold eight horses. For the few days until they reached Soviet soil, the transport moved slowly, adding boxcars at every town and not opening the doors for either food or rest stops to avoid people escaping. Kiev was the first stop inside the Soviet Union.

The Jews in Kiev find out that [the trains] carry Jews and the whole town was there and they threw us food and they were kicked by the soldiers.

Three weeks in the boxcars were followed by three weeks of boats and trucks, moving the twenty-five hundred immigrants who had refused

Soviet citizenship toward distant Irkutsk, north of Mongolia. Once the transport got into Soviet territory, the people were fed and the train stopped periodically so that they could relieve themselves, but Myer realized a significant change in their status.

When they let us out, everybody had to do something [go to the bathroom]. It didn't matter—a boy or a girl, one next to the other. It didn't mean [anything]. . . . You weren't anymore a man or a woman. You became an "it" right away. . . . You became converted to an animal.

In the town of Bodaybo, the center of the gold region in Siberia, the transports were handed lists of local villages. Families could stay together but their decision about their final destination had to be made immediately despite their lack of knowledge about the region. Deciding to leave their fate to the Soviet authorities "so at least I would not blame myself [for] what would happen," Myer and his family were sent to Sinuga on the Vitim River. Fortunately it turned out to be "the best place" because it housed the main government office and a very large bakery. Myer's family of ten filled their small, cramped barrack and therefore did not have to share space with another family.

When we came to Siberia, we got pushed back like a couple of hundred years. Not even electric. There weren't even lamps, there weren't even candles. . . . If they could get a little bit of fat, suet . . . they pulled a piece of cotton [from] the Russian standard jacket for winter . . . lined with cotton . . . and made a wick out of it. . . . If somebody had a pleated dress, they cut off half of it and made a fortune. . . . The [Russian] women gave away everything [for] a bra. They never saw [one before]. . . . The Russians, some of them, were very well off, but they never saw luxury. . . . There was a public bath. Every Saturday they heated it up and . . . when the Russian girls saw the girls' panties, you know, they were crazy about [them]. They all wear men's clothes. . . . They knew that we were more cultured than they are. . . . They practically worshiped us. . . . As a matter of fact, if it wouldn't be for them, there wouldn't be so many survivors. They helped us and they were so nice. I have no words for them.

Myer, along with the other young men, went into the surrounding tundra to lumberjack, returning to the village every other Saturday. Here, too, the people were helpful.

They helped us with everything, with the work. . . . The authority . . . gave us a saw and an ax and told us to go knock down trees. We didn't know how [but] we learned. . . . [The Russian workers] were glad to have us and they felt sorry for us. All of them had been sent [to Siberia] one way or another way. . . . They weren't just plain natives. . . . That doesn't mean that they were criminals. They were the same way that we were. . . . They were all in the same boat and they felt sorry for us. You know, if you came to a Russian house, he wouldn't sit down to eat without inviting you . . . and he shared with you the last piece of bread. . . . If they sent me somewhere and [it was] nightfall, the first house—I didn't care whose it was—I went there and I felt like home.

All the leaders [of the Russian workers] were Jewish. . . . The Jewish people, a lot of them, were sent as leaders, and a lot of them joined up voluntarily because if you came voluntarily you had priority. The secretary of the party . . . the local party there for the whole region . . . was a Jew.

I must tell you a little interesting story. . . . The first day we came there, two women, one young one and one elder woman, came to us and they were asking us in Yiddish . . . if there was anybody from the *chevra kadisha*. My mother, I told you, was [and so were two others]. . . . She asked . . . a favor. She has shrouds ready, and when she dies [she wanted them] to give her a Jewish burial. So they promised her. The next day this younger woman came [to say] she died. . . . They took her and gave her a Jewish burial and her son was there, and he said a beautiful *Kaddish*.[10] . . . A couple of days later, the paper comes out . . . and it said the secretary of the party, his mother died, and he gave her a Jewish burial. . . . They sent him away and nobody knew [where].

You were not allowed [to practice religion]. Nothing whatsoever. . . . There was a jail, too. . . . A rabbi there . . . they tortured him . . . and later they sent him away. I don't know where. . . . They caught him *davening*.[11]

[But] in secret, nobody knows. In secret, you can do everything. In Russia, you see . . . when you get caught doing something wrong, they don't say that you did something wrong. They say you got caught.

After the Germans attacked the Soviet Union in June 1941, some of the tension and restrictions on the refugees eased. Suddenly Germany became the enemy and Poland became an ally of the Soviet Union. Now the refugees could travel between cities.

[But] only in the winter you can travel. In the summer you cannot travel because there are no highways. . . . The mud doesn't dry out. . . . Everything gets paralyzed.

People died like flies [from] the diseases in the warm weather. In the morning we start to dig a grave because they told us that there were ten people dead. So we dig a grave for twenty and when it comes to close up the graves, they didn't fit in.

[10]Traditional prayer of mourning.
[11]Praying.

Once the snow falls and everything gets frozen, everything becomes alive
again. . . . The river becomes the highway. . . . Trains are going on the river. . . .
Tractors are going on the river.

Myer and his family moved to Bodaybo where he immediately secured
a job as a stevadore.

I'm sure God forgives me. I was a *gonif*.[12] You know, working as a stevadore
. . . I was like the . . . richest guy there. . . . On the first day [of work] I was [with]
Russian natives. . . . at that time there was flour being loaded and they looked
at me funny and I didn't know what [was wrong]. Second day . . . I went to
work and they started talking to me. They find out who I am. . . . They were
afraid in the beginning that maybe I am a spy. . . . They all . . . stole flour. . . .
In order to be safe, I have to steal, too. So they practically forced me to steal.
. . . They were equipped with . . . double pants and I wasn't equipped [so] one
guy took his belt . . . and tied [my pants] . . . so the flour wouldn't run down.
. . . I could hardly breathe, and the other guys poured it down [my shirt]. . . .
Mother . . . looks at the flour and she knew right away that I stole it. . . . She
started beating me and said, ''I don't want my son a *gonif*.''

But hunger and the Soviet marketplace eventually pushed these con-
cerns away.

One rule I made was just to use it for food, never for any luxury. . . . I brought
so much home that . . . a fortune was there. . . . Sometimes it was rice and sometimes . . . it was sugar [or] clothes [or] boots [or] soap. . . . Sunday morning was
usually a bazaar, a black market . . . usually near the railroad station. . . . People
. . . traded and they bought. . . . That's a way of life. If [the authorities] control
it, the whole country would be a disaster. . . . The black market keeps them alive.
. . . Even the big shot, he sold his things there.
   In Bodaybo . . . on the other side of the mountains, there were gold mines.
. . . If you caught [a man] stealing a piece of gold in the mine . . . he got punished,
he got ten years or so. . . . But at the same time there was a store. It was called
a gold redemption store. In this store you could get everything for gold. They
didn't take money. . . . If you came to the gold redemption store they don't ask
you where you got it . . . as long as you turn it over [to the government store].
. . . The same thing is with the bazaar. They didn't care.

In 1944, with victory in sight, the Soviets shipped Myer and the other
Polish refugees out of Siberia, west to Englestown on the outskirts of

---

[12]Thief.

Stalingrad. For their last two years in the Soviet Union, life for Myer and his companions was again slightly improved and they became more accustomed to the Soviet system.

First of all, we won [their] confidence. We were good workers—all of us. I was a *stakhanovite*. . . . A *stakhanov* was a guy [who] worked in a coal mine and in the coal mine a guy has to dig up so many tons a day. . . . He dug up four times as much . . . and every good worker who works four hundred percent [more] in any kind of work is called a *stakhanovite*.

Myer started out as a stevedore again, but his occupation changed in an unexpected manner.

They gave us a room . . . empty except a stove. . . . I didn't mind sleeping on the floor but Mother, I didn't want her to have to. . . . So I went to the guy to give me a bed. He said, "If I don't have [one], how can I give it to you?" I said, "Give me a couple pieces of wood and I will make it myself." . . . So he brought a crowbar, you know, and a saw and nails and he came with me and looked around to steal a couple pieces of wood . . . from a house. . . . He sat down and watched me make a bed, and when I finished . . . he said, . . . "You will work as a carpenter."
A carpenter had to do [everything]. So in the stables if something was broken, fix it, and if a window doesn't open, fix that. . . . If you needed nails, they gave you a crowbar and they said, "Go ahead."

Myer's mother died in July 1945. At that time he found a marked difference in the official Soviet attitude toward religious rites.

They gave me off eight days and for seven days I sat *shiva*[13] and I didn't shave. . . . The Ukrainisher . . . the head of the whole thing . . . says, "Why don't you shave?" and I said, "I cannot get razor blades," so he brought me a pack of razor blades . . . and I told him the whole truth . . . that it was a religious purpose . . . and he says, "I appreciate that you told me the truth." Later . . . I organized a *minyan*[14] in our house every day before we went to work. . . . They knew about it and I didn't care. . . . On Rosh Hashanah nobody went to work. . . . The brass came over. . . . They were watching what was going on [but] the war was over already so they got a little softer.

Life in general improved after the end of the war.

[13]Traditional period of mourning.
[14]Minimum of ten men needed for public worship.

If their situation improves, ours improves. That's like in a household. If you make a nice living, you give a child a bigger allowance and you buy better food, and the same thing was there.

As the Red Army began their advance into Western Europe, Myer followed the events in *Pravda*, given to him by his Russian superior, in accounts written by Ilya Ehrenburg.

He went with the Red Army and he . . . just wrote about what he saw . . . [like] the first news we had . . . about Babi Yar[15]. . . . He didn't have to exaggerate [anything]. . . . His articles made me realize that Stalin did me a big favor. He took me out of Europe. [Before this] I still had hope . . . that we will see [our relatives at home]. We were thinking that they are better off than we are. . . . But it didn't work out that way. . . . When we started reading Ehrenburg's articles, I was thinking I better keep my mouth shut. Who am I to complain?

Myer married a distant cousin in 1945, a young woman he had known from Poland who had been part of their group in Siberia.

Who would have wanted to get married [before the war was over]?. . . . You get so knocked down. . . . The feeling is . . . I am nobody. . . . Who am I?. . . I'm dead. . . . If you live a life like this, you don't care much about [things]. . . . You had no desire for sex. . . . Once we got out from Siberia, life was a little easier [but] in September '45 I got married [because] we knew already we're going out [of Russia] when spring came. . . . We didn't need a rabbi. . . . My brother-in-law performed the whole thing. . . . [Then] we went to the . . . Russian city hall and over there they [give] you a stamp. . . . It costs five rubles for a marriage license and twenty-five rubles for a divorce.

In the spring of 1946 Myer and his wife returned to Poland.

[But] the Polish people [were] very hostile. "Oh, you are still alive?" . . . Not only this. They kept on killing people. . . . They were worse than the Germans . . . because the Germans wouldn't do it if they didn't have orders to do it. . . . We had to live in groups and to keep watch for the [Poles] not to come and attack us.

They made arrangements to escape to Czechoslovakia under the protection of a guide.

[15]A ravine outside of Kiev in which ninety to one hundred thousand Jews were executed after the Germans invaded the Soviet Union.

We weren't afraid of the Czechoslovakian border guard because . . . we were running away and they welcomed us. But the Polish border guard, they would put us in jail. . . . We saw the border [guard] and a couple more guys set up machine guns. . . . The Czechoslovakian guards . . . started hollering for them to let us go and they didn't want to listen. . . . Finally we give [the Polish guards] everything. . . . A lot of people got killed that way.

The family worked its way across Europe to a DP camp in Ulm, Germany, where their two children were born, during their three-year stay.

We organized right away a militia, and I was [in it]. . . . You see, we were still [thinking] somebody's after you. They are going to kill you. . . . We kept the gates closed.

In addition to the defense and labor assignments which kept the camp running, they established a vital system of activities—social services, education, and recreation.

You did want to live a little. We stayed away from talking about [our experiences during the war]. . . . If you talked about it, life became miserable.

But thoughts and dreams did not stop. As soon as Myer found out about a DP camp nearby for children brought from Czechoslovakia, he immediately went to search for his sister's children.

They were there. . . . That was such a joyous day. . . . We were together again.

From the testimony of Myer Adler

10 *Henry*

Henry was sixteen when the Germans invaded Poland. His town in the eastern part of the country fell under Soviet control according to the Nazi-Soviet Pact, and his family made the difficult decision to accept Soviet citizenship and stay in their home. For two years survival seemed possible until Germany invaded the Soviet Union and Henry's family was exposed full-force to German control. Henry describes three years of terror—alternating between hiding and the watchful anxiety of freedom, death row in prison, beatings, and near-death in concentration camps.

In contrast to Myer's decision, Henry's family chose Soviet citizenship in order to avoid deportation to Siberia. Suppression of their religious and cultural practices and governmental control of the economy might be tolerated if it assured survival. The unexpected Nazi invasion of June 1941 swept over eastern Poland and caught the population totally unprepared. Panicked flight eastward could not keep ahead of the attacking Germans. Neither military preparations nor civilian evacuation had been anticipated. Under threat of another occupying power, some of the native population cooperated with the Nazis; some few risked their lives to help their Jewish neighbors.

Henry was born in 1923 in Jaroslaw, Poland, east of Cracow and close to the Soviet Ukrainian border. This oil-rich region of Poland had been part of the Austro-Hungarian Empire before 1918 and the Jewish population shared in the favorable climate of educational and economic opportunities. Henry's father had served as an officer in the Austrian army and his mother had completed her studies in an Austrian university and spoke German fluently.

While comfortable in both the Jewish and non-Jewish communities, the family was firmly anchored to its Jewish foundation. Various family members were active in different Zionist groups and Henry recalled with warmth the lively debates among them.

We used to have discussions, sometimes violent discussions. It was a lot of fun. We used to go Saturday to my grandfather's house, every Saturday . . . afternoon. We used to go to my grandfather, all the grandchildren were there. . . . It was very nice.

After World War I and the shift to Polish rule, the family experienced political and religious anti-Semitism though they maintained contact with their non-Jewish friends. Henry became increasingly worried over the events in Germany. He was growing up in a time of anti-Jewish legislation in Poland, and his parents' memories of more liberal times did not comfort him.

Being so close to Germany, we could feel this surge of anti-Semitism coming into Poland. . . . We had the refugees from Germany . . . Polish citizens who were in Germany . . . predominantly Jews [who] were deported back to Poland. . . . We learned from books and from them . . . what had happened in Germany. I was very scared about it.

Henry's father suggested moving to America, but his mother's roots held sway. "Why do I need America?" she replied. "I have America here." Even with the onset of Nazism and its encroaching influence in Poland, her early positive experiences persisted.

"How could this happen? [she asked]. The German people couldn't do . . . it." She didn't believe until the last minute when she died.

School became a daily battleground for Henry.

They used to call me a dirty Jew. They sang songs about the Jews. . . . As a whole the Jewish boys in the class were the better students . . . so there was jealousy. . . . There were always fights between us. . . . If I got hit, I gave it back, which meant it wasn't so bad. Of course, the authorities would never stand up for us, only against us.

I remember I was working all evening to make some Christmas decorations for school. . . . I worked very hard. . . . Since I was the first one [alphabetically] in the class, [my teacher started the grading with my project] and said, "Ah, it's nothing." He gave me a "3" which meant it was adequate which made me really mad. . . . Right behind me was sitting a boy who was a friend of mine . . . Polish . . . Karikula was his name . . . and he says, "Henry, I have forgotten my work to turn in. . . . Will you give me your work and I will turn it in instead of my work?" . . . He gave it to the teacher [and] he gave him an "A".

Henry described pogroms waged against the Jewish population of his town by peasants from outlying villages. During their Christmas vacation, university students joined them.

All the young Jewish boys stood in the doors of the houses . . . and wouldn't let them. . . . Sure we fought back. . . . We had our own tricks. . . . There was a time when the Jews were selling a lot of fish . . . because it was a Jewish trade . . . the fishmarket. So [the peasants] would bring their own fish . . . and they would make a lot of trouble. . . . [There were a] few known thieves in the town [who] would do anything for a dollar . . . a zloty. We gave [one] a zloty and he went and . . . poisoned all the fish. . . . [The peasants] didn't have anything to sell. . . . We fought back this way.

They [also] used to go [to] the synagogue when the Jews used to come in the evening [including] my grandfather. They used to tear their beards out and they used to beat him up. I remember I was in high school that time and there was a group of students who . . . all disappeared toward evening, and I was wondering, why do they disappear? And I found out. They used to go and fight the Jews. So we took care of them, too.

The family lived in the same apartment house which housed the Polish police barracks and had always maintained a good relationship with them. At the time of the German invasion, September 1, 1939, Henry was sixteen years old.

I was the liaison between the police and all the people, and I was going with the police in the police car, looking out at the destruction that the German airplanes did to the town. I saw the people blown up. . . . On September 7, I remember the . . . plainclothesman came in and he said to my father, "You better flee your town. The Germans are going to come in tomorrow morning. The rumors are they are killing the Jews."

Since it was understood that it was the men who were in danger, Henry, his brother, father, uncle, and several friends started off for the Soviet border. They stayed off the roads during the day since they were an easy target for air attack and traveled at night. They tried to avoid the anti-

Semitic villagers near the Ukrainian border as well as the invading German troops, but the westward push of the Soviet army forced them back home. Fortunately they found Henry's mother who, along with the remaining Jewish population, had been expelled from their home by the Nazis. They settled in the village of Lubaczow, about thirty miles east of their home and well within Soviet-occupied territory. The family was asked if they wanted to become Soviet citizens and stay in this town or keep their Polish citizenship and be deported to Siberia. They decided to take their chances and remain in Poland. Looking back, Henry questioned this decision.

Maybe [leaving Poland] was better, because maybe they [could] survive, you see? . . . I don't know whether it was a mistake or it wasn't because maybe my parents would be alive.

His father found work as a watchmaker and Henry attended "a very excellent trade school, one of the best Jewish trade schools in the whole of Poland. . . . It was a good place to be"—that is, until June 22, 1941. As soon as the Germans invaded, it was dangerous for the Jews to be caught on the street. They would check papers, confiscate rings and watches, take them to prison, or even kill them on the spot. The Germans were aided by both anti-Semitic Poles and Ukrainians whose activity was controlled under Soviet occupation but now "they had a free hand."

I was caught in one of these . . . raids . . . and I was [on my way] to the prison. Many of the Jews got killed. Just before the prison, I turned and walked on another street—just walked away and nobody saw me. I met a Ukrainian girl. She was very nice, and I said, "So let me go with you." She said, "Sure," and took me. . . . But two little boys who saw me . . . started to yell, "Oh, Jew! Jew! Jew!" So I said, "Shut up because I'll kill you right away," and they were afraid. They shut up and didn't say anything, and I went in a completely different direction with the girl. . . . She was a decent person.

The Germans immediately required that the townspeople register for work. Henry unloaded railroad cars but within a short time was deported to Jaktoruw to clean up the main highway to the Soviet Union for the German troops, "a murderous task." The men worked in frigid temperatures in the same clothing they wore when they were taken from their homes. They subsisted on coffee and a piece of bread in the morning, watery soup at lunch, and coffee at night.

A lot of people were actually starving. I knew a peasant, a Jewish peasant, who was always hungry. . . . One day he [went] to work and he froze to death . . . while he was working. He laid on the snow and he wouldn't move. . . . He couldn't do anything. He just committed suicide.

For the first time in my life I saw two people being shot—under my eyes. . . . Some people escaped from this camp, and there were two people who were sleeping on the floor of the camp. . . . The SS—Fox was his name—came around. He was mad. He said, "I must shoot somebody," and he shot this eighteen-year-old boy and a forty-eight year old man. I saw it . . . and I got sick.

[While] I was there I was beaten by the Germans. . . . They had the saws to cut wood and I was trying to make the saws sharper. . . . Well, you know, you work all day, I rested a little bit, and the Germans came in. . . . I got twenty-five hits.

Henry spent five months of the 1941–42 winter in this camp which was run by Ukrainians under German supervision.

They used to beat and shoot. . . . Their favorite torture used to be to come at night to inspect the cleanliness of your feet. . . . [If] they didn't like you, for example, they wouldn't like your feet. They're dirty according to them. They would take you out and give you twenty-five [hits].

They would also shoot anyone who attempted to go outside at night to relieve himself. As a result, in the sub-zero weather there were frequent instances of prisoners in the lower bunks soaked with urine which had seeped through the open wooden slats of the upper bunks.

Fortunately in March 1942, the Jewish Council from a nearby town was able to buy the release of five prisoners with funds supplied by their families. Henry was one of those released.

He returned home to find the town under Ukrainian control.

The only thing that helped us, our family, was my mother spoke very good German and whenever [the Ukrainians] needed something . . . to say in German to the authorities, they used to come to my mother and say, "Write me this and write me that," and my mother used to write them everything and would get a piece of bread, potatoes. So this was a little help.

In contrast to his experience with the Ukrainian camp guards, Henry found the neighboring Ukrainian peasants in his home village very helpful.

They were very good to . . . us especially. . . . We had very good relations because during the Russian occupation [when] we had some money and they used to come to us to ask for some food and some things like that, my mother used to give them all food and they remembered. There was one peasant . . . I remember when I came from the camp . . . he gave me his last potatoes.

Henry worked for these peasants for a few months—digging potatoes or any other job which would provide food for his family. But by the end of 1942 they were put in a ghetto in Lubaczow where conditions were terrible but life—for Henry—continued.

I met one girl, a very nice young lady. She was living near the school, where I used to go. So we became friendly and we used to go out together. Go out together? Where? There was nowhere to go.

Then in 1943, the family got word that the ghetto was to be liquidated.

One morning my mother told me to get out from the house because they were going to surround the ghetto and they were going to take us to the train. They were going to take us to Belzec. It was the gas chambers. . . . A half an hour later the Germans came. . . . They took all the Jews together. I wasn't home.

As to the fate of his family, Henry remained silent. As to the fate of the ghetto as a whole, he answered simply, "Everyone." It was not until much later in the interview that he added,

I found out the next day [about my parents]. I saw them going . . . to the train. . . . They must have died [because] as far as I know nobody ever escaped from this camp.

Henry hid in the home of a Ukrainian pharmacist until after the deportation. But the pharmacist, fearing that he would be discovered hiding a Jew, made plans to sneak Henry out of town to the home of the peasant who had given the boy his last potatoes.

I went to his house. I came about twelve midnight to his house and I knocked at the door, and he said, "Who is it?" I said, "Henry." So he said, "Wait a minute," . . . and he took all the children out from the room to the other room, and he brought me into the house. It was warm. He put me on the stove. . . . You could lay down on the stove. It was very warm. He said, "Lay down. Relax. We'll fix something. In the meantime, I don't want anybody to know that you're here because they are looking for Jews around here."

In the morning, Henry moved to the stable and the seven-year-old son of the peasant brought him something hot to drink every hour to keep him warm. Too poor to own a horse, the Ukrainian peasant accompanied Henry to town so that Henry could rejoin his brother in Lemberg (Lvov).

"I will take you to the village," [the peasant promised him], "so nobody will touch you." He gave me cigarettes, he gave me money, and he said, "Godspeed. I hope I will be able to see you."

Henry found his brother who was living in Lemberg under the protection of Polish Christian papers. He arranged for Henry to stay with a Christian family and Henry paid for a number of such hiding places since it was too dangerous to stay in one for very long. But "after being in 'freedom'— so-called 'freedom', I was caught again." He was put into Janowska, a work camp in Lemberg, from March to November of 1943. This camp, run by Himmler's brother-in-law—"a vicious murderer"— made Henry a witness to many more shootings and beatings.

I volunteered for every kind of work. . . . I was young, I was strong. I could withstand a lot. Food didn't matter to me—anything. However there were times when I wished I were dead.

One detail took Henry to the outskirts of town to clean up after the horses in a riding academy. Nearby a Polish family gave him bread and soup during his lunch break. In exchange, he cut their wood and did other chores.

One day, I said to them, "I won't see you anymore . . . because they're going to destroy us tomorrow." [The Polish man] said, "Why don't you stay with us?" I said, "Do you mean it?" He said, "I mean it." . . . So I stayed with them.

The following day, they took sixteen thousand young men and women out from the camp and shot them. The oldest was twenty-six.

Henry stayed with the family for about six months until they asked him to leave because the Germans were on the search again for Jews in hiding. He was recaptured and put into the Lacki Prison in Lemberg.

I was beaten up . . . by a young German because he asked me something [and] I didn't say "*Bitte*"[1]. . . . This was insulting to him. . . . The next day I was put into the death cell underneath the prison.

[1]Please.

His cellmates included two Jews from the 1008 Commando—a special unit formed by the Germans to dig up the graves and burn the bodies of Jews, as well as French, Italian, and Polish prisoners. There was a reward for catching a Jew who had escaped from a camp—a bottle of vodka. For catching an escapee from the 1008 Commando, the reward was a bottle of vodka and one thousand zlotys. These prisoners told him that they would all be shot. Within five days two were, but Henry and four others were returned to Janowska.

The five prisoners were squeezed into a hollow post to which the camp gates were connected [perhaps a guard station used by one man] and kept for several hours, until a young SS guard asked them if they were hungry.

I said, "Yes. I might as well die not on an empty stomach." . . . [He] brought us bread and coffee . . . and he came with a big sandwich with meat. He said . . . "Today is my birthday. Here. This is for you." . . . He was the sweetest man of them all.

The guard let them go to the latrine and gave them cigarettes and asked,

"Why did you let yourself get caught today? The Russians are already forty kilometers from the city." So I said, "The Gestapo caught us. We couldn't do anything." So he said, "Those bandits. . . . If I could do something for you, I would do it," but he couldn't do anything. I said, "What will happen to us?" He said, "You will be shot tomorrow morning."

Kept in the hollow post all night, Henry started to pray, when a young woman said to him, "Don't worry, Henry. This will take only a second. One shot and it's all over." The next morning, these five prisoners along with about twenty-five from the camp were taken to be shot.

They took us in the morning to the latrine again, because they didn't want us to soil the clothes. We went to the hole [an open grave] because they didn't have a crematorium. . . . They told us to undress. I started to undress. I was already in my underwear, and all of a sudden someone came on a horse, [an] SS man. He said, "Get dressed." I thought maybe they were going to torture us first. . . . We waited for the commandant . . . Himmler's brother-in-law. . . . [When he arrived, his] little dog came up to me. . . . He had a big dog and a little dog . . . and right away he knew me [from when I was in the camp in 1943]. He started to jump around me. I didn't know what to do. I didn't know what to do. . . . [The commandant] looked at me and said, "Henry, Henry . . . where were you?" . . . He knew me then because I used to fix his locks, everything. . . . I remember he hit me once with a pitchfork across the back. He almost killed

me. He was a ruthless killer. . . . [Now he asked] "Do you want to work?" . . .
It was luck. . . . The reason he let us go [was that] he had potatoes in the camp,
and in Poland they store potatoes over the winter. . . . Apparently they didn't
cover them very well and they were going bad. . . . He had a lot of soldiers to
feed . . . so he needed the Jews to make it good. . . . He let everybody go. . . .
This was the only reason.

So I said to myself, "Boy, if he lets me live, I will have to escape from this
camp. If it's the last thing I do, I'll have to escape from this camp."

After about three months, Henry was transferred to another job—
sorting the clothes of those who had died at Auschwitz. Ordered to
separate the clothes into "good, semi-good, and rags," the young Jewish
workers found a way to limit the profit the Germans could make from
this booty. "We used to tear it apart. Only a few clothes we used to give
back to the Germans." In the seams of the clothing, Henry and his friends
found arsenic and cyanide, hidden by those who had hoped to outwit
their captors and control their own deaths. They also found money.

Some of the money they offered to the Polish underground to get help
but "they refused everything, any cooperation with any Jews." Some of
it they used for food.

I had this girlfriend, and she had much more freedom than I had. She used
to go into town, to work in town. So I used to give her this money and she used
to bring bread and she used to bring something else to eat. She was as old as
my mother, but at that time, who was choosing? She was a girlfriend. She was
very nice.

But one day Henry's luck failed.

I found a gold coin, a little coin, and the boys told me, "Henry, you take
it." . . . so I took it . . . and completely forgot about it.

Later a German asked him to empty his pockets and the coin was
discovered.

"Take off your clothes. . . . All the prisoners, everyone has to see." There
were about sixty to seventy Jews . . . two to three thousand Poles and Ukrainians.
And they put me in a chair . . . a dining room chair. I had to put my head in the
chair [through the opening in the back], it was laying down, and they started to
beat me . . . and I had to count. I counted until I counted to one hundred and
eighty times—[it was] a leather pouch with two lead balls—until I went
unconscious.

He was taken to the barracks, but Henry was afraid to stay there since he could be shot for not working and returned to his job the following morning.

They started to beat me, these two Germans. They started to beat me with a pistol, a handle of a gun. They broke my nose, [they hit] both eyes, teeth. Blood was coming from all over, from every orifice in my body. Blood was coming, and I didn't say anything. They ordered me to say who was my partner [in taking the coin]. I said nobody was my partner, because I could imagine—one shot. . . . They would be dead. . . . They weren't touched.

Henry's brother, still living under Christian papers in Lemberg, learned of Henry's desperate condition. Through underground contacts, he arranged for Henry to escape through an opening cut in the wire fence. Henry was rushed to the Polish family who was already shielding his brother, and they started the slow process of nursing his wounds. Then, within a few days of his escape, the Russians liberated Lemberg. It was July 1944.

It wasn't a great event. I thought it would be much nicer, but it wasn't. . . . The Russians came in and they started to ask us questions. How come [we] stayed alive? . . . What did we do? Did we collaborate with the Germans?

The suspicion of his liberators aggravated Henry's already weakened condition.

I was sick, very, very sick. I was completely exhausted emotionally. . . . I was always so hungry. I could never have enough bread. . . . I dreamt about a piece of bread. . . . I was always sweating [on my] upper lip, sweating, weakness.

After a slow recuperation, Henry's spirit returned. He regained his Polish citizenship and finished high school in Cracow. He then went to Germany to a displaced persons' camp in Stuttgart, where he met his wife. After emigrating to the United States in 1949, he continued his education and completed his doctoral degree.

Looking back over these years, Henry recalled the times between his arrests.

The freedom, the uncertainty . . . this was the worst time. I'd rather be dead or in the camp, because in the camp you knew what was coming to you, what was going to happen. But in the streets, it was terrible. . . . Going down the street, walking on the street, you could never find what is going to happen in the next minute. Somebody would recognize you, because after all, I lived in this city. This was the fear that somebody would recognize and all of a sudden a German may come up to you and ask for your documents. . . . And especially [since] the Jews were circumcised, there weren't any but's and if's—once they [pulled] down the pants, you were done.

Living with such fear, knowing that his parents had already been taken to their deaths in Belzec, Henry had little faith that he would survive. It was when he was rescued from the edge of the pit, prepared for death and then asked if he wanted to work, to protect potatoes from the Polish winter, that he knew.

I said, "I'm going to survive." I knew I'm going to survive. Otherwise I didn't have a chance if I didn't believe in it.

From the testimony of Henry Altschuler

11 *Isadore*

Schooled for survival and independent action in a Polish orphanage, Isadore dodged capture by the Nazis and engineered escapes in the early war years to find temporary safety in Soviet-occupied eastern Poland. After Germany invaded the Soviet Union, he fled to the forest to join the Polish Jewish partisans and at the end of the war became part of the Soviet-controlled Polish army which followed the retreating Germans. His resistance gradually intensified—from refusing to work in potentially deadly conditions, to engaging in sabotage, to, finally, seeking revenge.

Thousands of small units of Jewish partisans struggled to survive alone in Eastern Europe because they could not join other, larger partisan groups. Threatened with deportation in their ghettos, these Jews risked starvation and savage reprisals in the forest from other partisans as well as Germans. Mortality rates were high. But for Isadore and other young people, it was a chance to survive that the older population and families with small children could not dare to attempt.

The years between World War I and World War II were hard ones for the majority of Polish Jews. The worldwide economic depression and a growing number of anti-Jewish restrictions made earning a living difficult, and some Jews tried to leave Poland for what they thought would be greater opportunity in Western Europe. What they found did not always fulfill their dreams.

Isadore came from one such family. He was born in Paris in 1920, the year after his parents arrived from Poland. France was not eager to have an influx of foreign-born workers, and so they had "smuggled" their way through the borders, paying contacts at pre-arranged points, and hoping that, once in France, a business would give them temporary working papers. Fortunately for Isadore's family, the Rothschilds hired his father and provided him with the work certificate he needed. But Isadore's father contracted tuberculosis in 1923 and was told it was terminal.

Those years in France, if you weren't rich enough . . . they didn't bury you in a Jewish cemetery or in a separate cemetery, only in a mass grave cemetery like thirty to thirty-two boxes. . . . There was a stick with pictures of all the bodies, all the dead people. . . . So my father was very much afraid, and being a Jew, an Orthodox Jew, he didn't accept the idea. . . . He was promised by the Rothschilds that they will put him in a Jewish cemetery, but he couldn't believe that, so he picked up the family and went back to Poland.

He died shortly after their return to Bedzin in western Poland, leaving his wife, seven-year-old daughter, and three-year-old Isadore. After four years of struggling as a seamstress, Isadore's mother remarried and bore two more children. Isadore's stepfather was abusive toward him and his mother "was forced to send me, to give me away, to an orphanage . . . the best thing that could happen to me."

Isadore was sent to an orphanage modeled after that of Janusz Korczak.[1] Isadore's orphanage had adopted Korczak's "charter"—an approach to raising and educating children which emphasized a strong moral code and stressed independent governing by the children themselves.

Children have to have a charter, how to act. . . . When I was eleven years old I was the president of the board, and I ran an organization, like a children's organization. I read the constitution . . . and we all had duties . . . to clean the rooms where we slept, to clean the bathrooms, to wash the dishes, to prepare breakfast, to give out dinner. . . . There were duties for every child to do. . . . Every year we had an election. . . . We had seventy-five to eighty children in the orphanage . . . so there were changes, but everybody had a duty. [Also we had] theatres. . . . I was awarded when I was eight years of age for playing in a theatre in a show, in comedy. . . . I have a very good sense of humor . . . and in a very short time I have been liked by people. And that's life—the way it's supposed to be. It's the way I was taught.

[1]Korczak, an internationally known Polish neurologist, writer, and educator, advocated a progressive approach to meeting children's needs. Later, during the war, he headed an orphanage in the Warsaw ghetto, and in 1942, voluntarily went with the children to their deaths.

The Jewish community of Bedzin supported the orphanage. According to Isadore, the Jews comprised about ninety percent of the town's population, including at one point its mayor. It was the wealthy sector that supported such institutions as the orphanage and other services to the sick and needy, much as the Jewish self-governing bodies, or *kehillot*, had been doing in Poland for centuries.

Every Thursday night, I would go after dinner . . . to the service building and one of the very wealthy women . . . a nice, outspoken [woman] was sitting . . . giving poor people money. And I used to stand at the door and let them in and let them out . . . and I can never forget. I was age eleven or twelve. . . . It was an honor to be picked.

At this same age, Isadore became involved in the Noar Tsioni organization—one of the many Zionist groups in Bedzin which prepared members to settle in Palestine. But Isadore felt his first responsibility was in Poland. After seven years of public school and three years of night school training as a tailor, he left the orphanage for his apprenticeship.

I was fifteen and I had to step out. . . . That's a shame that I couldn't use any better ways to be more educated in school, but time didn't permit. I wanted to grow up fast and start to earn and help my mother. . . . Hitler had already let *Mein Kampf* loose . . . and here I am trying to learn a trade and trying to help my poor mother. . . . You didn't think any more of leaving the country.

The anti-Semitism Isadore's family had tried to escape in the 1920's now increased in Poland under the Nazi influence.

They didn't march in the streets [but] Sunday morning they used to stay by the church and hand out leaflets, anti-Semitic leaflets against Jews. . . . They hired children . . . teenagers. They handed them out. [One] was my best friend and he said, "I don't mean you." He means the other Jews. . . . He didn't know what he believed in; he was told to hate the Jews. They were called to those rallies. . . . They used to have them in homes, and then when they went out, they were a little bit disturbed with the poison [of anti-Semitism] and if they saw a few little [Jewish] boys, they used to attack.

In 1936, Isadore tried to escape to France with a cousin. They got as far as Breslau before they were caught by the Gestapo.

Slapped in the face . . . we were told that they had their own pigs to feed and that they didn't need us and we were lucky that they let us loose.

When he returned home, Isadore found work in the shop where he had apprenticed as a tailor—until the 1939 Nazi invasion.

Within the next few days after the war started in Poland, they arrived in our town, very disciplined and very well-educated how to occupy the town. . . . [A Jewish shopowner was] scared to open the store . . . not that the Germans would take advantage, but that the Poles began to help themselves, to take the advantage that they waited for. . . . [They] helped the Germans to destroy all the Jewish efforts that they had put in [for] so many years.

Every day was another order posted through town—what a Jew has to give up and bring to the Germans . . . radios . . . gold or diamonds or anything they possess. . . . They formed a Polish militia and they started to catch Jewish young people and elderly people for forced labor in town, to dig trenches, to pick up bombs that didn't explode when they . . . invaded the city . . . things that were scary . . . that a Jew had to do under the supervision of the Germans with the Poles helping them.

I was nineteen. I didn't have much sense or maybe understanding or maybe enough leadership at the time . . . to resist . . . to fight . . . but I thought of a way . . . to escape . . . and it came to a time that I looked forward to it. Each time they rounded up Jews in town . . . for slave labor . . . I ran to the other city where my mother lived. If they start to round up over there, then I start to escape from one town to the other . . . hiding out, running. . . . I wasn't aware of them forming resistance in the city or surrounding towns, but I learned later that the resistance was formed . . . a very strong resistance in Bedzin because the city was predominantly Jewish.

Isadore tried to get his mother to escape from Poland but "she didn't want to leave. She had two children—I don't blame her." Nor would his sister and brother-in-law risk leaving with their children. From now on his decisions would be independent of his family.

In December Isadore was captured by the Germans and sent to work in a coal mine in Jaworzno, near Cracow, where he and the other young men had to unload coal from the wagons by shovel. After two or three weeks

I got together with a few of my close friends . . . and the four of us escaped. . . . I don't know how we did it, but one of the Germans got hurt. . . . What reasons and what manner and how it was [done] I found out later. It is not to repeat.

I couldn't go home now. . . . We made a deal that we were going to separate. . . . We were not going to run together. Everyone would find their own way. . . . I couldn't tell my friend where I am going and he didn't tell me, but we said we had to get out from here together. And we did. In the middle of the night.

I sent regards to my mother [when] I met friends in Cracow: "I am not coming home. I am saved."

Isadore escaped to Soviet-occupied Poland by wading through the icy December waters of the San River to the town of Przemysl.

[The Russians were] standing and waiting for us and shooting up over our heads . . . and they took us into a prison. . . . Now it's the KGB but then it was the NKVD[2]. . . . [I thought] maybe I will be safe if I tell them that I was a Communist in Poland. . . . [When] we came into prison I saw friends from town sitting behind the bars. . . . [One] hollered . . . out to me in Yiddish, "Don't ever tell them that you were a Communist, because they pick everyone that says they were a Communist and send them right to Siberia." They have a policy that if you are a Communist they don't need you here. You fight over there where you were a Communist. They interrogate you, they question you. . . . Lice . . . ate us alive. . . . We [had thought] that we would be saved [but] running away from one disaster, we came into another sort of a disaster.

For Isadore the interrogation was not very rough.

They knew the way you talked to them who you are and what you are. . . . I said I wasn't a Communist . . . and I said that my father was a tailor. . . . They let me out.

After a few days, Isadore and some friends went to Lvov.

We got a room. I don't remember how we got the room, but we all got into that room. Everybody was hunting for their own way to survive, to live, and we slept on the floor. . . . You worked for nothing, for a dish of soup. . . . Well, we found a way . . . to survive. . . . We did a little bit of business—odds and ends—with the Russian soldiers. . . . It was all illegal.

Then the Soviet authorities required everyone to register for work, and Isadore ended up in another coal mine in the Donbass region of Russia where all the laborers were treated equally. "Those years they didn't think . . . who is a Jew and who is not a Jew."

Here I see myself in an elevator going down four miles, three miles beneath the surface and they give me a coal crusher with a little shovel . . . and it happened

[2]Soviet secret police.

that I dropped one of my galoshes . . . and I went to pick it up. . . . Well, I figured I saw the dead in there underneath.

I said, "I'm not going back" which they tried to fight, but I resisted and I said, "No. I will not and you can do whatever you want to me. . . . Kill me." . . . I never did start to dig the coal . . . because I started to get a little bit more . . . guts. To start to resist, to fight. Not to make any emotional things, but just to refuse.

They were lenient. They weren't that strict. . . . They were civilian Russians. . . . Maybe they felt sorry [or] maybe they felt that I am not good enough. So I went up [from the coal shaft] and I start to mark the wagons that came up.

It didn't take very long and I decided that I will not make it. I figured that I would die young. It wasn't enough that I was young and I had strength. I had energy but I see that my strength is disappearing from me. . . . I was a tailor and I was trying to fight, maybe to go back to my trade. . . . And we picked ourselves up and we ran away from the mine.

Unable to return to Lvov because his name was on the police register, Isadore went to Rovno, which was also under Soviet control, and again did "odds and ends to survive."

I could have gotten in trouble in Lvov quicker than in Rovno because the Russian system in those years didn't work very well. If you want to move from one city to another, they lost you. You had to be on the run to get away from them. . . . The Russians had already started to pick up Jews, calling them capitalists, liquidating their wealth, whatever they built up over the years, and sending them to Siberia. . . . There was still an order not to call anybody Jew . . . but with the Russians if anybody was [what they considered] a rich man, they took him away.

Despite the restrictions, Isadore found it possible to meet secretly for religious services as well as for a resistance group which was readying itself for the dreaded German invasion.

When the war broke out [in June 1941] panic began again. I'm in the same shoes and the same hole as I was in Bedzin—in 1939. . . . People start to run, people look for survival, people become panicky. . . . Because they had already ghettos in Poland before, the Germans were already experienced. . . . Life became sordid. . . . Within two weeks of the occupation there was a ghetto [in Rovno] . . . and it didn't last long.

Immediately the Germans put Isadore in a slave labor detachment to build trenches against Soviet bombardment, and within a month or two

he escaped again with about ten men and a woman—one of the wives—
to the underground in the forest. Two days after their escape, the ghetto
was liquidated.

Isadore and his compatriots were led to the underground site by several
Polish soldiers who had escaped capture by the Germans and were now
working with the Polish resistance. But although these Polish partisans
helped them escape

we didn't want to unite with them. We didn't trust them. We always had to be
separate. We [even] hunted for our food [alone].

But they relied on information from these Polish resistance groups to
plan their eventual sabotage.

We started to get more knowledge from each other. . . . Then we start to learn
which forest this group is in and which forest this group is in. . . . There was
communication between the groups. . . . We fought together—in communication
[matters]—but not together.

The Jewish underground was young, primarily under thirty. "Younger
people had a little bit more courage." When they suspected that the
German invasion was imminent, they had tried to involve the older people
in the ghetto in their plan for escape.

[But] young people my age couldn't . . . persuade elderly people because if
someone was an elderly man, religious, he just waited for . . . you know, help,
and he couldn't have the same effort as a young fellow. A lot of elderly people
did try to lay there and hide out. The Ukrainians were hiding people.

But for these young partisans, the forest was their chance for survival.

[I was] living in the ground in a bunker and covered up with trees with grass,
[with the war] right above me, right over our heads. . . . In the same forest . . .
maybe five or six times, the Germans occupied and the Russians occupied . . .
fighting, chasing one another forward and back, and we were in the ground. We
couldn't show ourselves in the daytime. We could only go out at nighttime from
the forest, going to little towns, countryside, to survive, to get food . . . dog food
. . . anything we could have gotten to make survival. . . . We lived like pigs.
There were no facilities. No, that wasn't pleasant.

Yet at the same time, their faith persisted.

We still believed in God. We said prayers sometimes. . . . We knew when a holiday was. . . . On Yom Kippur we had a fast. We didn't eat. We didn't have [anything] to eat, but we didn't eat. . . . I remembered my father's *yahrzeit*[3] and I said *Kaddish*. We had a *minyan*. . . . Other people were free believers. No one interfered with the others.

The native population was aware of the presence of the partisan groups in the forest.

But they didn't know the hideouts. They didn't know where we were. We couldn't trust. We had people going out—they looked like gentiles—going out to hunt for food. They had connections with Poles in certain places, with Ukrainians, to deliver the food in exchange for gold, whatever it was, and one didn't know . . . from where are we coming . . . and where are we going. . . . And this was all peformed at nighttime, in the middle of the night.

By the end of 1942, the war was beginning to shift as the Soviet Union advanced against the Germans.

When Russia started to succeed in the war against Germany, we already became stronger with more people . . . about forty-five men . . . and we were in time to help to destroy German property. . . . We already had more power, more ammunition . . . to strike against Germans . . . destroy German bridges. . . . Maybe I wasn't involved too much in dynamiting, but it was help. There were more courageous people than I am. I was a little naïve or maybe too young to take a rifle to start to shoot to kill but, if it came to it, you have to do it.

With the advance of the Soviet army in 1943, the partisan group dissolved. Isadore proceeded to the Maidanek concentration camp in Lublin, now liberated from German control. In the same barracks, until recently filled with prisoners, the Soviets were training a Polish army unit to pursue the retreating Germans.

On his way to Lublin, Isadore felt that he was the first Jew to pass through some of these small towns since the deportations.

I picked up the Jewish *siddurim*[4] and *chumoshim*[5] from the ghetto . . . They were burned, half-burned . . . and I used to burn them . . . and buried them [according to tradition]. . . . And then, I enlisted myself in the army.

[3]Anniversary of the death of a parent or other close relative, marked by prayer of *Kaddish*.
[4]Prayerbooks.
[5]First five books of the Bible and prophetic passages.

[At Maidanek] the ovens were still there and there was a big ditch with people covered with lime that the Germans didn't have a chance to burn. . . . [A Pole] . . . looked at those people and he said, "See, all the Jews are here" and I picked up a cross from the ditch and with that cross were nun's clothes . . . and I said, "Is it Jews, or was it meant for you, too?" And he had to shut his mouth.

I didn't hide it at the time that I am a Jew . . . but on the other hand I was on the look-out. . . . I will be suspicious until the day I die. . . . [But] I had to be united [with them] for the only purpose that I wanted—to take revenge.

By 1944, Isadore had completed a six-month course in anti-aircraft. He was then a front-line soldier in Polish uniform in an army unit under Soviet supervision. He went into Warsaw twice before August 1944 when other Poles in Warsaw staged an uprising against the Germans.

[But] the Russians told us not to cross the border. Stay back. So the Germans killed [Poles] the way they did with the Jewish ghetto.

By early 1945, Isadore was sent to Lodz where he was able to get information about Poles who had helped the Germans.

[They had] tried to help the Germans destroy the Jews and we found out about them. . . . The time came for revenge. . . . It was an illegal procedure [but] I had a little bit of power. I wore a [Polish] uniform and I found more Jewish soldiers already in the army. I [also] found Jewish officers in the Russian army . . . and they already knew [what] Hitler did and they started to feel with us. . . . I think I started to feel better [when I took] the revenge which we did.

We went out every night for a little bit pride. We had a list, Poles giving us lists of all those names. . . . They were glad to give us details because their civilians couldn't do much. . . . We went out two, three soldiers at night. . . . We did use guns but I had to close my eyes and ask God for forgiveness [for] what I have to do. Because of being a Jew it was a hard bite. It was the worst thing in my life . . . to see what I have to do. . . . It was my commitment. . . . That's why I enlisted myself. I didn't have to enlist myself to become a volunteer . . . but I did it because of revenge. I wanted to do it and I did it. . . . As it went on, I felt satisfied. We didn't touch . . . German [civilians].

As they moved on into Germany, Isadore moved back from the front line to work with the officers reading maps. He observed,

The Russians behaved themselves abnormally with raping German women. . . . The Polish soldiers . . . robbed but they didn't behave themselves as . . . brutally. We [the Polish soldiers] had orders: we couldn't do it. . . . Stalin gave out orders not to touch the [civilian] population, the ones without the uniform, but the revenge was there. . . . The same things that the Germans did to the Jewish girls . . . they did the same thing.

Returning to Bedzin after the war, Isadore knew that none of his immediate family had survived. But he located his wife-to-be and her sister. Released from the army but not given a pass to leave Poland, Isadore and the two women, along with several cousins, smuggled their way to Germany through Czechoslovakia. Eventually they arrived at a displaced persons' camp in Degendorf, Bavaria, where they stayed until their emigration to the United States. In the DP camp,

we talked [as] individuals and we talked in groups. Everybody contributed their problems. They shared their experiences and we talked, but we start to live, to live life. . . . We got married. . . . We have dances, we form theatres . . . Yiddish theatres, cantorial concerts. We start to bring life back to survival.

[Talking about what happened during the war] didn't hurt us anymore. . . . We were affected already. . . . We were trying now to connect the past problems with the future. . . . It helped to relieve and unite us . . . thinking about the future that we shouldn't stay in Germany. [It helped give us] strength and that's where we start to smuggle out people . . . children, to Palestine. It gave us courage.

From the transcript of Isadore Hollander

12   *Nathan*

Nathan was thirteen when he escaped the German massacre of all the males in his Romanian village. His remaining family was confined to the Czernowitz ghetto for the rest of the war, where Nathan defied both Soviet and German control in the struggle to ensure their survival. Numbed by constant exposure to death from starvation and disease as well as arbitrary and sadistic murders, Nathan confronted the enemy in fearless escapades, unwavering in his belief that he would outwit death.

Romania had been notably anti-Semitic long before World War II and refused to recognize many of its Jews as Romanian citizens. On top of pre-existing civil and economic disabilities, the Romanian government willingly collaborated with their German allies in persecuting and deporting Jews, especially in territories Romania annexed, such as Bukovina, where Nathan's family was ghettoized. Despite the terror surrounding him, Nathan found a few precious allies—other boys as eager as he to find some enjoyment and means of surviving their war-torn youth.

Nathan's small home town of Unter-Stanestie was in northern Bukovina, part of Romania at the time of his birth in 1926. Most of its sixty to seventy families were Jewish, including a wealthy landowner, professionals, merchants, and a small number of poor who were aided by an active *kehilla*.[1] In the surrounding area lived Ukrainians, Poles, and Volksdeutsche.[2] Nathan's father operated a family store which had man-

---

[1] Jewish community organization.
[2] Volksdeutsch (s.), Volksdeutsche (pl.), a person of German descent living in Eastern Europe.

ufactured and sold fabric and clothing for two generations. He had been educated in Vienna and registered for medical school before his plans were disrupted by World War I when he enlisted in officer's school and served as first lieutenant in the Austro-Hungarian army. But despite his social and economic status and his allegiance to his native country, Nathan's father had a strong interest in Zionism dating from his exposure to Theodor Herzl, one of its first exponents, in Vienna during his student days. Though his father considered himself modern Orthodox, dispensing with the traditional beard and *payes*, Nathan followed the orthodoxy of his mother and grandfather, wearing *payes* till the age of thirteen and studying Talmud with his grandfather, a highly respected *tzaddik*[3] in this deeply religious town. But at the same time, Nathan joined Betar, one of the many Zionist groups in his area:

I was too young to understand exactly what Palestine meant to the Jews at that time, but I liked that organization with their songs and their stories and it gave me a feeling of patriotism with the Israeli flag. . . . It was like a dream for us at that time.

The family had a comfortable relationship with their Christian customers.

Mostly our customers were Ukrainians and we had a very good relationship because my father was a very humble man so most of them—I would say ninety-nine percent of our customers—never paid cash. . . . They always had credit . . . so we had a good relationship.
Anti-Semitism [existed] always . . . [so] we as Jews, unfortunately . . . always used to be bent . . . with our heads down, not up. Submitting. We knew we were second class, that this was not our country.

In addition to his religious studies in the *cheder*, Nathan attended the public school together with Christian children and a totally Christian teaching staff.

Jewish teachers . . . were not accepted. . . . We learned prejudice . . . day out and day in. . . . Every day we had prayers in school where we were all standing up . . . and we were forced to kneel too, except they made the cross and we did not. But they were always bringing up . . . about how Jesus Christ was crucified by the Jews . . . and when we had recess . . . we used to get beaten up by them because they said, "You killed our Lord . . . " and I said, "I didn't. What did

[3]Pious, righteous man.

I do? I am innocent. I don't know anything about this.'' So then we started defending ourselves and then we used to have fights . . . and most of the time we were victorious. . . . I was known as a bully and I used to beat up a lot of them. . . . You had to take defense in your own hands because no one would defend you. I was too young to understand . . . what would follow later.

I am a human being the same as them and suddenly they hate me. There was a fear on the holidays. . . . On the thirty-first of December they used to dress like a goat [with] two horns representing the Jews, the devil. There was always one other one in the back dressed in a national costume with a long whip. And he used to whip [the goat] symbolically, to disperse the devil [for] the coming of the New Year. . . . [The goat] used to then jump up [as if he were] suffering pain and [the one with the whip] used to say, ''Curse you Jew, curse you Jew.'' . . . A scapegoat. . . . That exactly.

At that time the Jews were always closing their doors. They didn't let us out from the house because of the violence, but I used to watch from the windows.

Good Friday was [also] a very frightful day for us because at that time the hate was more outspoken. Jesus was crucified. . . . I remember that even in school they used to teach [this] in front of us. We were also punished in school many times—standing, I remember, for nothing . . . in a corner and [at other times] hot, dry corn was thrown on the floor and we had to stay on our naked knees on the corn with our hands up. . . . It used to dig in you.

In 1938 when he was twelve, Nathan was sent to Czernowitz to a gymnasium[4] where the big-city atmosphere meant less anti-Semitism, more friends, and his first exposure to parks, movies, and streetcars. But in 1939 after the start of the war and the signing of the Nazi-Soviet Pact, the Soviet troops began to occupy their designated share of Eastern Europe and by 1940 had marched into Nathan's home town.

We had already come back to our town because we knew that something [was happening]. . . . They marched in with a couple of tanks and troops came in and they threw flowers and candies to the kids and everybody welcomed them. . . . Nobody opposed them. The Romanians went back to Romania. . . . Actually we welcomed them [the Russians]. At least the Iron Guard[5] and the Jew-haters were not going to hurt us. . . . Because of the repression and the prejudice, many Jews had joined the Communist Party. . . . It was a movement which considered everybody equal according to Marx and Lenin. There is no religion. . . . Everybody that is a human being is equal . . . the rich and so on. So many Jews had no choice. . . . If there are two devils you choose the best one.

[4]Upper secondary school.
[5]Ultra right-wing and anti-Semitic fascist organization in Romania.

Immediately all property was nationalized, including Nathan's family business. His father was appointed manager of a beer hall.

My father had to work because if you didn't work you were a parasite, a germ . . . a vagabond.

Nathan returned to the public school, but under Soviet occupation, "we felt more secure." Teachers no longer made anti-Semitic remarks; instead it was anti-religious propaganda.

That's how they brain-wash you. It had an effect on the little [children] who were only five or six years old. [As for] us, we knew that it was only a comedy. . . . [There was] still anti-Semitism [but] not official.

Concerned that the Soviets would see his father's previous bourgeois status as a merchant as a "bad spot in my biography," Nathan decided to apply to a school in Kharkov to become a train engineer.

To me that was adventurous—to travel on a train all over Russia, thousands and thousands of miles. . . . There were four of us . . . two Ukrainian boys and two Jews. . . . We went to Czernowitz to take a test and we were all together and we had nice uniforms and food and [the chance to] travel and [the idea that] they will train us. . . . My mother was very much against it and my father too, but I figured that it's an adventure and sometimes you don't think about your consequences in the future.

The boys were accepted for admission, but Nathan never attended the school. The Soviets, they soon learned, were "relocating" the bourgeoisie.

In May, they started to deport Jews from our town . . . the rich people. . . . We were on the list. . . . They deported every night like three families. They came in a big, black truck . . . and took them out in pajamas, the way they were, and they loaded them up. They could take nothing with them. . . . And the next morning you found out that the house is sealed and they have gone . . . to Siberia. We were on the list because we had a big store and a beautiful home and so on. I think they deported no more than seven or eight Jewish families, also non-Jewish families, rich Ukrainians, too. . . . If on the twenty-second of June 1941 the war hadn't started, we would have been deported [within] two or three days. . . . Every night we would wait for the truck to come and the knock on the door that we are going to be deported. . . . We would have been better off. . . . Those who were deported to Siberia . . . who didn't die from starvation and cold survived [and] after the war came back. . . . Maybe it would have been better.

When the Germans attacked Russia on June 22, Nathan's family stayed put.

Some Jews from our town . . . maybe five or six families, were smart enough to leave . . . and go to Czernowitz because it is a big city. They had some intuition, some gut feeling, that it is not good to stay here. . . . We never thought about that. We had friendly Ukrainian neighbors for years. My father had in that town two Ukrainians who [were with him] in the Austro-Hungarian Army in the First World War . . . so he figured, "I have nothing to fear. I didn't do anything." And no one feared. . . . I was . . . adventuresome . . . as a boy and in 1941 I was exactly thirteen years old.

The Soviet authorities retreated within the first few days and the Ukrainians assumed command, patrolling the streets and restricting everyone to their homes. Nathan recalls with painful clarity that Friday, the last Sabbath he would spend with his whole family.

My mother made the regular Shabbos. She made *challah*[6] and *cholent*[7] and gefilte fish—not gefilte fish, regular carp—and soup and chicken. . . . I looked out . . . the venetian blinds . . . and I see the Ukrainians going back and forth. They didn't have cars or jeeps but they were running back and forth and everyone was armed with a rifle or, if they didn't have a rifle, they had a tool—a machete, a long knife, a spike, or anything— and back and forth and back and forth and no one dreamed what would happen. But we were in fear.

We didn't sleep all night. We were all watching [out] the windows off and on. Maybe we fell asleep for a couple of minutes or so. Saturday morning we couldn't go to the synagogue. We couldn't communicate with anybody. . . . Saturday around eleven o'clock or twelve o'clock in the afternoon, we looked out the window and we saw Jewish families marching—mothers, fathers, sons, and daughters and so on and behind were two Ukrainians. We saw other families going. . . . Everybody has an escort. . . . My father says, . . . "I don't think anybody will come after us because I didn't do anything wrong." And then when he looks out and sees one of [the Ukrainian guards] who was his buddy in the army . . . he said, "He!" Well, four o'clock in the afternoon . . . this same man who was my father's friend . . . came to our house . . . and he apologized in a nice way. He said, "I am sorry, but I have orders. . . . Every Jew has to register. And anybody who isn't a Communist—I know you are not a Communist— doesn't have to be afraid. . . . I have an order. I must do it. I feel bad, very bad, but I must do that." . . . We wanted to take some clothes with us and food . . .

---

[6]Twisted loaf of white bread eaten on the Sabbath.
[7]Casserole of meat, potatoes, and vegetables eaten on the Sabbath, kept warm from the day before.

and he said, "Nothing. You will be back in five or ten minutes. You don't have to worry about it." . . . So we left with what we had on.

I will never forget that walk. As we were walking, we saw [that] from everywhere families are going. No one talks to each other. They are scared and frightened. Pale in the face. They are going. No one knows. They have to register.

They were taken to the courthouse where they were surrounded by Ukrainians armed with First World War arms, hunting rifles, machetes, pitchforks, and hatchets.

One of the guards . . . outside was one of the young men, so-called friends, who was supposed to go with me to that special school. . . . I approached him before we went in. . . . "Why is everybody armed? We didn't do anything." He said, "I am sorry. We were friends but I can't do anything. That is the law. I have to listen to others."

We waited there. . . . Each window had bars, heavy bars. . . . It was five, six, seven, eight o'clock and outside we saw . . . them coming and going in two's and three's. They own our lives and we didn't know what would happen but we knew something was not kosher. They said, "Later on everybody is going to be taken to the city hall to be registered." So at twelve midnight, the heavy door opened and one Ukrainian came in, followed by two in the back, with a list and started reading, "Chaim Feldman and his two sons Moishe and Yankel, registration, male." It doesn't matter if he was three or four years old. Male. They went. Another group came in. "Shutzman and his son." No females. And this is the way it went.

My mother had some intuition . . . so she threw me on the floor . . . took off her shawl . . . and threw it on me and she sat down on me like a bench and . . . also two other ladies. . . . I didn't want to, but she pushed my head down.

But Nathan's father did not have the same premonition.

Nothing . . . It was like two or three o'clock in the morning and when we looked around there were no men anymore. Only women. Some were crying. The last was my father. [And then they called us.] . . . "Schneider, Yaacov and Natan." My mother says that I went already. So he says, "All right." And my father took off his wedding ring and gave it to my mother and he kissed my mother and my sister and he couldn't kiss me because I was under the blanket. . . . He says, "Don't worry. I have nothing to fear. I am innocent and I will be back very soon with the registration papers." That was the last we saw my father.

No one remained from that group. I was the only survivor [along with] one man [who] hid himself between a chimney and the wall [and] another one [who] crawled behind a partition. . . . The windows were open. It was in June. You could hear from far away . . . terrible screaming and yelling like hyenas, howling. . . . It was a mile away and we could hear it and I will never forget it. . . . Then it quieted down. About four o'clock the sun came out. One guy came and said, "Tomorrow we will take the women for registration . . . and you will join your husbands."

The women were told that the men of the village had been deported to a labor camp and when they asked, "What was this hollering and screaming," the guards answered, "Oh, dogs."

We never realized. For the next two years, we thought they were going to come back.

Eventually they found out the truth.

A survivor [of the massacre] who had seen all of that . . . wound up being in a concentration camp and survived and told the whole story. . . . Apparently he was hit by somebody who felt sorry for him and [told him], "Make believe you are dead." He fell down in the ditch, with dead bodies on top of him. [He later reported] they didn't take all the men together. . . . They were taken individually to about half a mile away to a big, big barn. There, they were stripped completely, of everything—their jewelry, clothing, completely naked—and . . . they were escorted by two Ukrainians. . . . [Then] they knew where they were going. . . . There was already a ditch that was prepared . . . in the bottom of a mountain . . . and there [the Ukrainian guards] said to those henchmen, "Here is yours. Do whatever you want to do." . . . Very few were shot because they had no bullets. Most of them were hacked to death. . . . They say about . . . the rabbi, they cut his head off and they spiked it up on a big, big stick. They were dancing around like wild Indians.

Some of them they put in sacks, in cotton sacks, and tied the sacks. . . . Years ago they used to hit the grain with two sticks . . . until the [kernels] fell out. This is the way they used to beat that [person] in the sack until he was massacred. How my father died, I will never know.

It was all organized by the Ukrainian intelligentsia, the educated men, the postmaster . . . the priests. . . . Eyewitnesses told us after the war and during the war . . . that they assembled the entire town. All the women, children, and everybody had to come like to a festival to watch that massacre. Some of them were crying, weeping, crossing themselves, because some of them had some humanity in them.

On the morning after the massacre, the Romanian troops marched in and ordered a halt to the killings. They deported the surviving women and children to Czernowitz where the other remaining Jews from the region were concentrated in a ghetto. They traveled on foot along country roads and through villages where they were stoned by local peasants. Now controlled by the Romanians who were under German supervision, they were given yellow stars and Jewish identification papers and awaited their call for another "resettlement." The Jewish community leaders were ordered to make up the list.

They only left behind those [who were] needed for defense. My uncle [my mother's sister's husband] was a textile designer. They gave him an exemption and he took us in as his dependents—my mother and me and my sister . . . and we were exempt . . . temporarily.

The population of the ghetto diminished daily—through deportations, dysentery and typhus, and starvation. The Romanian authorities provided no food and the ghetto community was left to its own resources.

Those Jews that came from surrounding [towns] . . . came with absolutely nothing as far as money or clothing . . . but the Jews who were right from Czernowitz . . . they had a chance to take some of their belongings which they later exchanged with the non-Jews. The exchange was done . . . at nighttime through the barbed wires or on certain days that the non-Jewish were permitted to get into the ghetto. . . . [They came for] trading or just to visit. . . . It was a tragic comedy to see how the Jews lived.

The prisoners of the ghetto held on to each day—trading, smuggling, scrounging for potato peelings to supplement their rations from the Jewish community soup kitchen. Some were able to pay *bakshish*[8] to get their number on the deportation list pushed back for several months. Meanwhile people clung to precious war reports on short-wave radios, joined political movements from Communist to Zionist, organized Hebrew schools, fell in love and got married.

Nathan was assigned to a labor unit ordered to reconstruct a bombed bridge. The constant threat of danger was leaving him numb.

I saw there—personally, [as an] eyewitness—executions. . . . They took an elderly man who could not lift, who was incapable . . . made him kneel down and they shot him in the back of his head. . . . It was like, "So what? So they shoot you." Life didn't have any meaning at all. Danger and adventure, day by day.

[8]Bribe.

For Nathan and his friends, adventure became a way of blocking out so much death. Despite reports that people attempting to crawl under the barbed wire at night were shot immediately by the Romanian patrol, they did it.

We had a special spot under the barbed wire near a tree where we used to crawl out the other side. . . . We met at a place on a little hill with trees outside the city and we used to play cards there. . . . It was very stupid at that time because our life was in danger, but as a young boy you never think the danger is close to you. What can happen? [It was] like from the dark side to the light side.

We had lookouts who watched for the guards. And we used to walk out the other side and take off our yellow stars . . . and we didn't have any papers or documents in case we got caught. We posed as non-Jews, sometimes mingling with the population on the street. I [still] have a picture today with a friend of mine, parading in one of the biggest, nicest boulevards like . . . Chestnut Street or Walnut Street [here in Philadelphia]. . . . The danger was they would close up the streets and ask for our papers. . . . Many times I was stopped but I could wiggle myself out [of the situation] by speaking the German language, by lying to them . . . insisting that I am a Volksdeutsch . . . and smiling at them straight in their face. . . . We were daring young boys. We didn't realize [how] close death was or what danger was because we went through so much in our lives. . . . Maybe life didn't have any meaning or [else] it was stupidity. . . . [But] to walk and feel free and feel freedom which was a forbidden freedom. . . .

Nathan became close friends with a boy whose mother was Jewish and whose father was Christian and a colonel in the Romanian army. This family lived outside the ghetto. Pro-Jewish and anti-German, Nathan's friend dreaded his father's pressure to become an officer in the Romanian army. The young Romanian and the Jewish boys from the ghetto shared both worries and adventure.

We swore friendship between us and we trusted him. He never betrayed us. He [told us when] the Germans and the Romanians were getting slowly defeated on the Russian front. . . . He also told us how Jews were massacred [by the troops] on their way through . . . Russian territory.

Even their attempts at having fun together had unforeseen consequences.

So one day he says to me, "Do you want to go to the movies with me?" . . . and I said, "But how am I to go in? . . . If they catch me they will kill me." He said, "Don't worry. I am going to give you a silver swastika. You'll put it on here and if you get stopped by the SS or the Gestapo, just say '*Heil* Hitler' and you go through.'' ... I was a movie buff and they showed cowboy movies [so] I went with him to the movie. It happened that the movie was a very repugnant ... propaganda movie called ''Jude Süss.'' [My friend didn't know this. He meant] to entertain. ... I remember it showed how the Jew with a long nose tried to cheat and rape a German, blue-eyed, blonde-haired girl, Aryan, and so on. After the movie, I remember that the people were so instigated that they stood up and said, ''*Heil* Hitler! Kill the Jews!'' ... When we walked out from the movie, there was the Gestapo asking for papers. I didn't have any papers but right away my friend said, ... ''Say '*Heil* Hitler' and say you forgot the papers. You are a Volksdeutsch.'' As a matter of fact, I used to wear short pants and I had very short hair, crew cut. I looked like a Volksdeutsch. ... My heart actually stood still. ... They got suspicious and my friend ... showed his papers and they figured we were together and he is Christian. Why will I be a Jew? So they let us go. I came home and I told my mother and my aunt and they all said, ''You are not normal. You are out of your mind. ... You are risking your life.'' And I said, ''That is what life is all about.''

Another time Nathan and a Jewish friend were caught on the main street outside the ghetto, ''walking, seeing nice girls walk by. I was young. ... '' Arrested and accused of being Soviet spies, the boys were forced to clean up a clogged washroom with their bare hands under machine-gun guard. They protested that they were Volksdeutsche but this time they were not believed. Again Nathan's friend helped.

My friend ... influenced his father who was a colonel in the Romanian army. ... ''Friends of mine are accused ... of being spies. Can you [use] your influence?'' ... If he called us Jews or non-Jews, I have no idea. ... All we know is they came into the cell and they opened the door ... and we were scared because we know that the Germans used to have a trick. They say, ''Go,'' and they shoot you in the back. So we came out slowly, not running, and as we came around the corner, we ran like we had never run in our life. ... We never stopped until we couldn't breathe anymore. Later we met with our friend and he told us that he asked his father how he did [what] he did. [His father explained that] the Romanians were actually running the country [and] the Germans were only there like supervisors ... so apparently he had some influence.

But the Jews also experienced direct German power. Once Nathan and his fellow prisoners in a forced labor unit were stopped by two German officers in a jeep.

"Line up, all of you" [and he] pulled out the fifth or sixth or seventh [person].
. . . He starts to count and you gamble, like playing at the casino. . . . Our hearts
were down in our pants.

They took them away. . . . Later we heard the machine-gun fire. . . . It was a
sport and he feels like killing a couple of Jews. Nobody is going to punish him
for that. When we came back to the ghetto, I remember the daughters, the
mothers, the girlfriends used to wait at the gate and they saw how many less
came back . . . and they started crying.

After the Soviet victory at Stalingrad in 1943, the Romanians feared
Soviet occupation, particularly massacres by Soviet troops because of
Romanian complicity with the Germans. As a result, some of the Jews
in the ghetto were released if they were involved in defense work. This
included Nathan's uncle and his family. Although they moved a block
outside the ghetto walls, they remained under the watchful eye of the
Romanian government. They still wore the yellow star and had strict
curfews and they could shop only when the non-Jewish population was
done.

Those few hundreds of Jews who succeeded living outside the ghetto were
under constant fear and under constant pressure. . . . They had to produce.

However, the Soviet army was advancing to Czernowitz and the Romanian leadership left, leaving the city in the hands of the Germans.

Then started another chapter of terror. . . . They killed a lot in the ghetto [but
for] those who lived in scattered houses like us, they didn't have any lists or
addresses. They just went by what non-Jews were telling them. There is living
a Jewish family, there is living a Jewish family, and so on. . . . Whenever they
found out where any Jews were living, they were taken away. Where . . . or how
. . . no one knows because I don't think anybody had the courage to investigate.
[At first] the SS took over the whole city and I remember they were in black
uniforms and they had that skull on their heads and they were patrolling in those
small jeeps and armored trucks. . . . In the apartment house where we lived there
was a big courtyard and one day three armored trucks and a jeep came in. . . .
We were hidden all in the basement and looked out . . . a small little window
. . . and here they are. . . . We figured it doesn't make sense to stay there . . . so
I walked out and I started a conversation with them and they did not know that
I am Jewish. . . . I said . . . we are Volksdeutsche. . . . They had biscuits and chocolates and they were looking for schnapps. . . . We had several bottles of . . .
regular rubbing alcohol . . . and mixed that with kimmel [from] caraway seed
and made from one bottle of 100-proof alcohol . . . four or five bottles of

schnapps. . . . I made an exchange with them . . . the biscuits and the chocolate and petroleum . . . for the schnapps.

I made conversation with a young . . . Austrian and he was telling me that he wasn't SS. . . . He knows the war is coming to an end but he is innocent. He said, "I am from Austria. I have a wife and two kids and I don't want to fight in this war but they forced me to get into it." He didn't know that I am Jewish. . . . We had that exchange and, as a matter of fact, we had a couple of laughs and a couple jokes.

He told me that Hitler is *kaputt*, the war is *kaputt*. The Bolsheviks are coming and they are going to pay back what [the Germans] did to them. . . . In a way, I felt bad for them because they were scared, they were very, very scared. . . . The funniest thing, the irony of that, is that he apologized to me that he didn't want that war, that he was forced into the war because he was an Austrian. [But] no one forced them to go to the SS. . . . You had to volunteer. . . . How many Jews and non-Jews were killed by the SS . . . I never asked him. . . . How much he had on his conscience . . . that is another story.

On the last day of the German occupation, the SS drove throughout the city with loudspeakers warning the population that they were going to blow up the warehouses filled with food and supplies. They did not want the Soviet soldiers to find anything of value when they occupied the city. They told the people to take what they could before the explosion. Despite his family's objections, Nathan decided to get what he could. The war was still on and they could not depend on the Soviet forces to provide them with supplies. Again, dressed in his short pants with his crew cut and his perfect German, Nathan posed as a Volksdeutsch, joining the streams of townspeople heading for the warehouses.

In that commotion [I was very] much confused. . . . I don't think there was any food left [because] the Germans needed it. There were mostly goods. In that warehouse that I found . . . were shoes. I grabbed two big bags—the Germans supplied you bags, big, big bags like army duffle bags. The bag was bigger than me and I started stuffing in. I didn't realize they were all lefts. The people were coming in. They were grabbing, and I took about a dozen shoes that were all lefts. It is funny but tragic. I took hats from the boxes and stuffed them in. Then the most valuable thing I took was yarn for shoemakers, waxed yarn. . . . I grabbed a couple of boxes of metal horseshoes. . . . Also I took some bales of . . . silk.

Near me was another guy who was a non-Jew, a Ukrainian . . . from Czernowitz. He was doing the same thing. We were both taking nonsense but we were stuffing [our bags]. I looked outside and . . . it is unbelievable. People have gone mad and are dragging things. Then came the loudspeaker that says, "You have one more hour."... The dynamite was already put under those warehouses. They just have to light a fuse. So finally, I and that unknown stranger who was my age—I a Jew and he the non-Jew—became friends. And in our walking together out from there, he said, "You are Jewish?" and I said, "Yes. I'm Jewish." He said, "Well, in a short while we will both be liberated."

The two boys were late getting out of the warehouse and suddenly found themselves the only ones on the road. They struggled with their bags to get to safety when they heard the explosion, saw the smoke, and felt the earth shaking. In the confusion of the retreat, an SS patrol stopped them, suspicious of the heavy bags, especially the sound of the heavy iron horseshoes which they thought might be ammunition. Again Nathan claimed he was Volksdeutsch and his new friend remained silent.

He could have said, "He's a Jew," but he didn't. [Instead] we said, "Look, we are Volksdeutsche and we don't have any parents.... We have nothing. This is all of our belongings."... So he opened the bags and he saw inside... all those shoes... so he said, "Go ahead, but run."... We came to a crossroad. [The boy] lived in a different section and he said to me, "Good luck, good-bye," and he took off.... As I was going around the corner, here is a jeep passing by with four SS and they stop right away and all of them get out their automatic machine guns.... "Hands up! Stop! Who are you? You are a Russian spy! You're a Jew!" And I said, "No, I am a Volksdeutsch" and I made a salute, the awful salute which actually saved my life.... I made them believe ... I had a sick mother and my father is fighting in the front [and] we have to survive.... Finally they decided to let me go... and [then] I encountered one more [unit] exactly four hundred yards from my house.

My uncle, my mother, and my aunt were looking out from the basement. You could hear the artillery.... You could see the flashes of the light in the sky.... I would not let those bags go. Those were my bags. Somebody else would leave those bags and run for his life, but I had to have those bags.... I could not show him where I live because they might follow me and find everybody there, so I figured I have to out-maneuver them. [It was] the same story.... They said, "Fine. All right. Can you run?" And I knew that old saying.

I figured that I would take that risk and I grabbed the two bags. I was tired already from lifting those bags so I was dragging them actually... and I was running zig-zag... for my life.... I looked back and the jeep disappeared, so what I did, as I was passing in front of our courtyard, I threw the two bags in. I threw one bag in and then the second. For fear that maybe they had followed me and would discover everybody, I ran around the bend to the corner, into a courtyard, and from there I climbed two different fences and [crawled] under fences [until] I landed in the yard where I lived.

When I walked in, the reception that I had there was unbelievable.... "You are out of your mind. You know you could be shot? You could have brought the Germans to us. . . . What do you have here? A dozen left shoes!''

But then they saw the silk, and from trading that cloth, they were able to buy supplies for the next half year of Soviet occupation.

The Soviet army, still in pursuit of German troops, formed a civilian militia in Czernowitz to keep order and control vandalism and provided them with weapons.

I found out that some of my friends from school had survived. They came to my house and they had automatic Russian weapons and they said, ''Natan, take it and come with us.'' My mother right away took a white handkerchief and put it on my head and said that I have a terrible headache [so] I cannot go. . . . I said, ''No. Don't do that. I am not a coward. . . . I have to take revenge for what happened to our people, to my father.

About seventy Jewish youths, under the leadership of a Russian partisan, were divided into patrols to protect the city. Part of their job was to search out Germans in hiding or Ukrainians who had aided the Nazis in massacres such as Nathan's family had experienced. But after three days the Soviet army brought in their own men for this job.

The Russians had them all killed. . . . [They] had a code. . . . Any SS or Gestapo should not be taken prisoner alive. . . . I understand that some of the bodies were hanging for twenty-four hours right there in the square. It wasn't . . . a pleasure to see that because we . . . felt sorry even though they were our tormentors. We felt sorry because we figured maybe one of them is innocent and maybe he has a wife and children.

Now under official Soviet control, the community had new orders: children attended Soviet schools, businesses and homes were nationalized, all males over the age of sixteen were inducted into the army to ''fight the fascists to the end.'' Nathan was now eighteen.

My mother was very scared because she had lost her husband. . . . She wanted me alive and she knew that . . . we didn't mean [anything] to the Russians. . . . To sacrifice 100,000 soldiers for their aim . . . meant nothing to them. . . . But I went very proud. . . . I wanted to go because I wanted to take revenge.

Nathan joined about thirty young men, both Christians and Jews, in a demolition squad trained to defuse mines so that the troops could safely enter the field.

To me it was a big adventure at that time. . . . I had no fear. We were taking out [each] day . . . at least a couple of thousand mines. As soon as you take the capsules out of the mines, the mines were not in danger anymore. I remember we used to have . . . mountains of those mines that were not dangerous because the capsules were out. . . . But the capsule itself . . . they were dangerous. . . . I collected a lot of souvenirs and being a soldier we had a satchel and day by day I filled it up full of those capsules and didn't realize that I was sitting on a time bomb. . . . We used to take some of the mines and put them up for target shooting. . . . Every single day we had casualties. . . . I remember that suddenly, in the back to the left, boom, an explosion and all that remained was pieces of flesh or clothing on the trees and there was nothing to collect. But it didn't scare us. . . . I was a little afraid, but it didn't scare me. This was going on for months.

As time went on, Nathan found his goal shifting toward survival rather than revenge. Problems with desertion in the Soviet army meant that troop transports were guarded with bayonets.

We resented that very, very much. We felt that we were prisoners, forced to go, sacrificed for the war. . . . I want to fight the Nazis, I want to take revenge, but not that way. I did perform my duty under different circumstances, but they didn't have any trust. . . . [Now] my aim was to escape.

As we came to the railroad [to go to the front] . . . the commotion started— trains coming back with prisoners of war, some wounded Russian soldiers, and tanks and supplies and trucks and troops going to the front. . . . I made believe I was going to the bathroom. . . . I relieved myself for a half hour waiting for the train to leave . . . and finally the train took off. . . . I had to report because I was in uniform and I just couldn't walk away. I went to the Kommandatur and I reported and said, "I lost my train". . . . He said, "No problem. On the next train you join them or we attach you to somebody else. . . . Wait here." . . . People were coming in and out . . . and after about a half hour he walked out and left me alone in there and another officer came in . . . in a very good mood, smoking a cigar made from newspapers and cut tobacco and whistling. . . . I said, "I am waiting to go back. I am on furlough." And he said, "You cannot go on furlough on an army train. . . . You just have to go on your own. . . ." So I walked slowly through town, but I had a paper with me that I am a soldier [so that] if somebody stops me, I am going to say that I lost my train.

Afraid to jeopardize his family, Nathan did not return home but went to a cousin's house where he burned his uniform. But within a couple of weeks he was picked up on the street and forced to re-enlist. He was immediately placed in an infantry regiment, the only Jew among Poles, Ukrainians, and Russians.

And one guy sitting across from me says to me with a smile, "You know, you stinking Jew . . . when I come to the front line . . . I will be behind you and instead of shooting the Germans I will shoot you first." . . . So I made an excuse to go out, like to the bathroom, and I went and reported it to one of the officers . . . and he said, "Disregard it." He was a Jew-hater too, so I figured there was no sense going to somebody higher . . . because higher may be the same way. They don't care. . . . So, I figured: escape. . . . Some were playing the guitar . . . all kinds of singing together and everybody knew that tomorrow morning at eight they would be all gone. . . . I am free to go. No one stops you. Not realizing that when I walked out from there another dozen were [leaving] after me, Ukrainians . . . all young guys. . . . For some reason, we had some confidence in each other. . . . We had the same fate, the same destiny at that time.

Breaking through a locked door, they discovered a sentry patrolling on the other side. The empty street was already bright with the early morning sun. Waiting for morning traffic to camouflage their escape, they shook hands, wished each other luck and one by one, melted into the crowd.

After a period of hiding, Nathan went to Bucharest under an assumed identity and joined Zionists who were helping Jews get to Palestine. After the State of Israel was established in 1948, it was Nathan's turn to leave.

Thinking back over the end of the war, Nathan recalled a scene still vivid in his memory. During his last months in the Soviet army he saw a train of German prisoners of war stopped, its doors opened for fresh air.

They were all young—fifteen, sixteen, seventeen years old. They were fresh from the front. Some even had mud on their hands and feet and faces and they were bandaged. . . . The population that were standing on the outside were cursing them: "You Nazis, murderers!" And I will never forget: German prisoners, SS, youngsters were standing here on a Russian train going to their destiny . . . stood up all of them and said, "Long live the Führer! *Heil* Hitler!"

The population was outraged, so they started throwing stones and everything at them, and they closed right away the doors. . . . I felt bad because they were young and they were doomed. . . . Wasted life. I was satisfied with one thing— that they won't do anymore what they were supposed to do. . . . They are in good hands, because if they had fallen into American hands I am sure they would have given them chewing gum and blankets and chocolates and in two years they would have been out in the street. But not the Russians. So it's a shame that all of the . . . Nazis, . . . criminals, SS, did not fall in their hands.

I understand when they went back into Russian territory, those in grey uniforms were taken away. They were actually separated from the SS. The SS were all killed by machine guns. They [also] used to bring the cattle trains into . . . the mountains and they didn't even kill them. They used to dump them down into the ravine.

Revenge is revenge.

From the testimony of Nathan Snyder

13 *Chayale*

Chayale Ash Fuhrman, prominent in the Yiddish theatre, recalls her child-hood in Romania as the daughter of Yiddish actors. European market towns welcomed the excitement of the theatre troupe arriving in covered wagons bringing music, costumes, and popular biblical and folk themes to the people. Caught in territory newly acquired by the Soviet Union in 1939, the theatre troupe temporarily joined with the Soviet Yiddish theatre company until the German invasion of the Soviet Union forced them to flee to the east. Chayale spent the remainder of the war trying to adapt to the strange life of Soviet collectives in Uzbekistan near the Afghanistan border.

Yiddish theatre was born in Romania at the end of the nineteenth century largely due to the creative efforts of Abraham Goldfaden, called the father of the Yiddish stage. Composer of music and lyrics as well as scripts, he introduced biblical operas, historical drama, comedies and revues, as well as adaptations of Yiddish short stories, and his model was followed by other theatre troupes such as that of Chayale's father. The material was directed toward the common people, the Yiddish-speaking people of the shtetl or small town of Eastern Europe, where the emotional, responsive audience thrilled to the rich culture of Yiddish theatrical style. Although the plays have been reproduced in other countries, Chayale's memories encapsulate a time and experience in European culture which were com-pletely erased by the Nazis.

Born in 1920, Chayale grew up speaking three languages—Yiddish at home, Russian in the street, and Romanian in school—since her home in Kishinev in the province of Bessarabia was Russian until 1918 and Romanian until 1940 when the Soviet Union took it back. Her family had lived for generations in this large Jewish community where there was a vital intellectual and cultural climate which fostered such projects as the professional Yiddish theatre. For Chayale and her family, this was their life's work.

She lived with her grandparents during the school year but traveled with her parents during her summers from the age of two.

I slept on a big . . . wicker case . . . and in this was parts of scenery and little wigs and all kinds of costumes, and they used to make my bed on this.

By the time she was six, she had a speaking part in *Kiddush ha Shem* by Sholem Asch and could taste the exciting flavor of her parents' Yiddish theatre troupe.

I remember times we were traveling with wagons, covered wagons . . . like you see in the West, the pioneer, and my father used to be with the children. This was the way of traveling. . . . The town could have five hundred Jews, but they came to perform in that little town. . . . The streets were not paved. They used to come at night to the theatre with lanterns and the mud up to here, but still they came to the theatre. Because theatre was a part of Jewish culture. They couldn't be without it.

I remember . . . that a big star from America . . . came to a little town, and it was raining and it was muddy, and he couldn't come here in his nice shoes and his nice coat, top hat—you know, the old time actors—and he couldn't come to the theatre. The mud was up to his knees. So people came from the town and they made a little bench from their hands . . . and they were carrying him to the theatre to have the performance that night in the rain. . . . This was real life. Working people, the younger people, the people who were dreaming for a better time, they were eating theatre. This was their life. This was their school. . . . [Sometimes] a group of actors performed . . . vaudeville-style or comedy, musical comedy. . . . For another kind of audience . . . the more literary ones . . . biblical plays . . . and fantastic music . . . fantastic biblical operas.

[The troupe] was a cooperative. . . . Everybody got the same. . . . In that time it wasn't . . . a special one to make the scenery and a special one to do the makeup. It was a group of actors . . . doing everything for themselves. My father—he would come in the theatre in a little town not finding any sceneries and take newspapers and put them on the back of the wall. And in one minute was a forest or a sea or whatever has to be the background of the show. . . . They used to wear . . . the starched front of the tuxedo . . . not the whole shirt . . . only the front, you know. . . . There were times that one pair of shoes was worn by the same two or three actors, if they were not at the same time on the stage. . . . It was *real* theatre. I mean with all the heart. . . . An actor gives all his soul for that.

In the summertime, the troupe performed in open air theatres in the larger towns of Romania. In the winter, they went to the smaller towns and used the largest building available—the fire hall, a wooden hall where movies were shown, a brick building used for wedding receptions. They advertised their performances when they arrived in town.

A poster sometimes written by hand was put on a little wagon, and the wagon was traveling around the town for the people to read. And there was another system. They call it a "caller". . . . Sometimes you hear the caller say, . . . "Tonight, eight o'clock, you can see the Yiddish performance, 'The Witch' from Abraham Goldfaden, and don't forget, at five o'clock they are heating up the *mikva*[1] and Yossel had a son . . . " and the same time he had in his hand a big basket with bagels he would sell . . . walking the streets. They were really characters that have disappeared from life, and it was fantastic.

When Chayale was ten she attended The Professional School for Girls in Kishinev during the winter months, a program supported by the Jewish community, where she learned sewing as a trade in the morning and studied her academic subjects in the afternoon. Everything was taught in Yiddish, with French as a required second language. By the early 1930's, just before Chayale entered her teenage years, she joined her parents' theatre troupe full time, though she continued to be tutored in Hebrew and Gothic German. But now the idealized summers of her childhood were gone. The climate in Romania was changing.

[Now] started the era of anti-Semitism. . . . The air was already filled with this kind of thing in the '30's, so they start [not] allowing renting theatres to Jewish theatres. A printer wouldn't print posters for Jewish theatre, so they were written by hand. If the police would come, they say that it was a benefit for a poor family or a benefit for a poor bride to marry. . . . So, we used to prepare leaflets or tickets . . . "This night is a benefit for this and this cause", so if the government comes they know it's a benefit, not theatre.

Within a short period of time, the troupe could not even use the excuse of performing for a charitable cause. They needed a complete façade.

[1]Jewish ritual bath.

[Then] theatre was performed in tea houses. People came to drink tea and in the moment that the show was to start, they put down the tea. . . . In case somebody comes from the government [the play stopped and the] people started drinking tea.

In the summer of 1940, when Chayale was twenty, the Soviet Union took parts of Romania, including Chayale's home district of Bessarabia, while other Romanian territory was given to Hungary. Jews were blamed for these decisions, the mounting anti-Semitism became violent, and many Jews tried to flee. Chayale and her family tried to return to their home base in Kishinev, believing that Soviet jurisdiction would be the safest.

[There was] no train we could go on. Full of military people, full of peasants moving from place to place . . . it was a chaos not to describe. So we rented a wagon with horses . . . and we start, and in every town, all the roads were closed with wagons, with horses, with wagons with oxen. People were moving from place to place, thinking they don't want to be [here] . . . they don't want to be there. . . . And the roads were closed. No food. . . . And I remember we start selling certain things to give us a little food. . . . What has to take six hours by train took us a week to . . . arrive in Kishinev.

Right away the stores were emptied out of food, clothing stores were emptied out of clothing, because the Russian people start coming over . . . and buying out everything. I remember women used to buy nightgowns and put them on as dresses. When we saw the first time this kind of thing, we couldn't imagine, [but] the Russian people didn't have [anything to buy] on the other side.

Fortunately for Chayale and her family, the Soviet government formed the Moldavian Yiddish State Theatre—an ensemble of one hundred twenty people including dancers, makeup specialists, artists, and seam-stresses. Now there was immense relief that there would be work and financial security.

An actor has in mind . . . I have only to give my talents and the rest the government will take care of. . . . But it wasn't this way at all. They were dreaming that it would be this way. Because you cannot perform what you want, you cannot interpret a part like you would like to, because the director . . . usually a Russian . . . has to put on you the "how to do it"—to be in the line of the country.

It was restricted. First they organized right away like a branch of the Communist Party in the theatre. . . . Everyone had the feeling that he has to watch the next one. . . . The head of the theatre would call people, actors, saying, "How was the other actor? Is he good? Is he talking about something?" . . .

You feel always watched. . . . You know what it means, the atmosphere in general? . . . the suspicion?

Then you had to do the show they want. . . . They forced us to bring out in every show the social problem. If there wasn't one, you had to interpret it in such a way that there is one. . . . In a show, if a scene was in a factory of *talesim*, a guy is killed—they are making a strike and he is killed. They want to bring in the whole *talis*[2] soaked in blood [to show] what the rich people did. . . . For an actor who performs for the sake of art . . . it was a very hard thing to do . . . to think politics in the time that you are rehearsing. . . . They eliminate plays that . . . have religious contents, a play that looks positively on, let's say, an owner of a factory. . . . They wouldn't allow certain writers [of plays dealing with Jewish culture]. . . . They forced on us translations in Yiddish from Russian plays.

[The Soviet Yiddish actors] were not knowledgeable of the Yiddish literature. . . . They were speaking . . . Russian . . . even knowing that [the other] actors do not understand. . . . They were competitive. . . . Theatre has to be the mirror of life. They didn't think about it this way. They were acting . . . mechanical. Nothing came from their soul. [With some of the younger Soviets we] would become friends, but with the older ones it was impossible.

Chayale wanted to study directing under the famous Jewish actor and director Shlomo Michoels in Moscow. She started a correspondence in which he agreed to give her a job typing to pay for her studies. But the German invasion of Russia in June 1941 stopped these plans. Kishinev was bombed and the theatre company left hastily on a train going east, hoping that the Soviet Art Department would protect them. Over one hundred fifty people, trying to stay together, pressed themselves into a cattle car.

It was a panic in this train. . . . The bombs were falling. . . . It started . . . pulling us away from the station and some of the family relatives were [still in] the station and the families were lost. . . . They had gone down to bring some water.

Moving further into the Soviet Union, the troupe was shunted from station to station to let troop and equipment trains through. They finally arrived in Kharkov in the Ukraine after two months only to discover that the Soviet Art Department had also fled with the German advance. The theatre troupe was not permitted to travel further.

[2]*Talis* (s.), *talesim* (pl.), Jewish prayershawl.

They say . . . the fields are full with grain and . . . with corn. The men are on the front [so] all the people from the trains . . . all the theatre . . . should go down in the *kolkhoz*—*kolkhoz* means cooperative settlements . . . to help the people, the Russian people, to take down the grains from the fields.

There we found out the first time what it means really—hate for the Jews. The villagers from the town, from this place, mostly the women, start talking, "Jews, you are not in the front fighting for us. You stay here in the back. . . . You are hiding from the war." They didn't know that no Bessarabian, even young, was taken in the army. [The Russians] didn't trust from the occupied territory to take in the army. One woman said, "I will scratch your eyes, you stinking Jew." This is what she says to me like this with the two fingers in my eyes. Why? . . . She wouldn't hate a government that sends her husband to the front, but she gave all her hate to the Jews.

For Chayale and the other young people, working in the fields was not so difficult,

but seeing my mother . . . the actress, the prima donna, working on a tractor . . . and my father [on a] horse and other actors . . . first grade actors carrying . . . working . . . I felt so sore inside. . . . I saw my mother standing in a big hole, you know, with manure, and they add water and they are stamping with the feet and making bricks from that. . . . I suffered, not for me—I was young and I could work. And for me getting up and working with the girls and boys together, singing when we were working, it's a different atmosphere than seeing old actors and actresses doing labor on the fields where . . . they wouldn't dream about it, they don't know it. . . . Their bodies are not used to this kind of physical work.

Chayale was assigned to pack and carry hay by hand.

I remember, all the time I felt hay on my body . . . scratching . . . itching, in my eyes, in my hair . . . always this dust of hay on me. And I remember I came home (little huts . . . for refugees) it was a big barrel, very big barrel with water and I used to go in this barrel and make my bath after the work. What it was, for a young person . . . it didn't matter. I was in a barrel, the moon is shining outside, and [I am] sleeping like a log . . . but for the older actresses, it was terrible for them.

After the harvest, the troop moved on to Tashkent, hoping again to link up with the Russian theatre.

We met tens of thousands of people around the station. . . . They are like ants. Sleeping in the station, sleeping under the benches, sleeping in the garden outside

from the station. They were in lines. Everywhere you look you see lines. . . .
People were dressed up with everything they had.

At this station, a government representative informed them that the
Russian theatre was disbanded. They were now on their own in the
province of Uzbekistan, near the Afghanistan border.

Chayale and her family went to another *kolkhoz*, this time harvesting
frozen cotton that had to be separated by hand. Here they met some other
Jewish families who had fled from the German invasion.

They were used to the life of Russia—the black market, to the stealing . . .
selling, buying—things we didn't know. . . . They know that they have . . . to
bring a bottle of vodka or a carton of cigarettes . . . to the head of the *kolkhoz*
and [then] they didn't have to work so hard. . . . This was a way of life . . . things
we didn't know. We knew it very well later on in 1942 and 1943, but in the
beginning we didn't know.

Living conditions were primitive and food scarce.

They . . . gave us every day three hundred grams of bread and a certain soup
. . . more water than soup, but this is the way it goes. And a refugee in Russia,
you could see . . . on the waistline near his belt . . . this container with a spoon,
always tied down [so he wouldn't] lose it. We used to make the containers from
tin cans. This was the symbol of a refugee.

Then Chayale discovered that the head of this *kolkhoz* was stealing
sacks of rice and other grain, concealing it in a hole in his hut, and having
big parties with drinking, roast lamb, and pilaf.

I decided that I have to go . . . and tell the truth. . . . So, I went there with
another son of our actors, together. We were the young rebels. We saw what
was going on. . . . I told them. But we decided we . . . will never return to the
cooperative again because . . . maybe he will take revenge on us or it will be
bad for our families.

Chayale heard later that the head of the *kolkhoz* was arrested and
imprisoned. She and her mother left the cooperative.

I tell you what happened to my father. . . . His nerves were very sick. Usually
women [survived] . . . a lot easier than the man. For a man it is very hard to
change his routine life, and it is everything. A lot of suicides among men. . . .
They didn't see a way out. . . . I was young. I didn't have shoes. I went barefoot

three miles to dance. . . . But fathers, they couldn't swallow the whole thing.
. . . Life without theatre was nothing for him at all. And he shaved his head. He
didn't have anything to wear. And he went into the markets. . . . He was stealing.
. . . He was not rational at all. . . . My father got . . . dysentery . . . so we took
him on a wagon . . . to the hospital. Later on we found out . . . that my father
died. They put him in a grave with fifty other people who died because there
was an epidemic. . . . He was forty-eight years old. . . .

Still I survived with my mother. We had malaria. We suffered terribly from
malaria. I remember the first time I saw my mother naked in a bath. . . . My
mother was a nice, plump . . . actress, you know . . . and I saw her naked and I
start crying and I run away from the bath. . . . My mother looked the same way
[as] the people when you see them from the extermination camps. Some people
don't think that being . . . in Russia in a labor camp . . . was like it was.

But there were precious moments as well. Once Chayale's mother was
able to steal a white sack used for packing cotton.

She put it around her body [when she was in the bathroom at the cooperative].
She could be shot . . . because everything was . . . for the front. Everything for
the war. . . . Nothing private. . . . And she brought it home. . . . I took a pencil
. . . this violet pencil, and I mashed it [into] a powder and I boiled water and I
colored the sack violet, purple. And by hand, I made myself a little dress. This
was my dress I went dancing in . . . and on my feet I had a pair of slippers which
I made . . . myself from pieces of cotton . . . and I didn't have any socks. But I
was young. Nothing mattered, only to survive.

In every town refugee young people meet. They used to sing songs, play the
balalaika, dancing. . . . I knew that three kilometers [away] it's there, a group
that you can meet young people. . . . So with this violet dress, like a jumper
style, with cotton slippers, fabric slippers, I went dancing. I remember one day
I got an attack of malaria in the middle of the road. I . . . lay down on the road
. . . for half an hour, until I stop shaking, and then you are all sweat after the
shaking stops from malaria. . . . I wiped my face, I straightened out, and I continued my way to the dance.

In the beginning of Chayale's stay in Tashkent, her relationship with
the Uzbek villagers was very good: "They respected us, European. They
considered themselves Mongolian, Asians . . . Their religion was Islam
before the Russians came in" and they kept much of their culture as well
as their mosques.

The door's always open. If a stranger passes by, he can come in and if they
are eating at that time, they ask him to the table. Sometimes I was looking [to

find] smoke. So then you know that they are eating. So you know you are always welcome to go to eat with them together. They are eating from one plate of pilaf. . . . Everyone is drinking the . . . herb tea from the same cup . . . like a bowl. You're sitting and you're giving to the other one around the table. And the wife is never together with the husband. Like in Islam. She is near the oven. She feeds the kids . . . but when a new person came, even a woman, they still invited me to sit together with them.

But there was a change once the Uzbeks came back from the front.

They [the Germans] are killing *their* Jews. There has to be a reason for that. They start introducing the hate they got on the front. They start looking differently. . . . A young Uzbek said, "Why do they say in Germany that every Jew has a long nose?" Stupid questions, but they came already with the poison inside them because they were together with the soldiers, there on the front, from Germany.

They stopped inviting you. You could pass by and if you went in, they said, "You wish something, you want something?" and sent you away. . . . The tone was a little different. For myself, it was a little different. Why? I invented an idea to survive. They put little hats on the babies. Usually their babies have . . . skin problems. . . . The head is shaved . . . and they used to [cover] them up with little bonnets. I took a skirt from my mother, I tear it apart, and I sew little bonnets. And at the top, little buttons or something. And I used to take this little bonnet when I saw the smoke coming out [of their chimneys]. "I came. I brought a little gift for you for the baby." Then they invited me.

It was this skill in sewing, learned before the war, that gave Chayale entrance to a sewing cooperative. Here she surpassed the quota of shirts she was to turn out on the foot-pedaled machines to get more bread. Then her ease in learning the Uzbek language enabled her to attend a textile school.

And I'll get food in the school [I thought]. The best place to go. The mind . . . didn't work. . . . At night, at day, when you are awake, only food. This is the only thing a person could think of.

When the authorities discovered that Chayale could read and write Russian as well, she was assigned as a clerk in a steel mill, checking to see if people were performing their jobs.

It was so hard for me to make a report on a deserter. . . . I used to tell them, "If you have to do something, if you have to go to market to sell your cows . . .

whatever you have to do, tell me. Tell me so if the head will ask me . . . I can say you asked permission. . . . If not, I have to make a declaration as a deserter.'' So the Uzbeks loved me enormously. . . . One Uzbek brought me some eggs. One Uzbek peasant brought me, like a little handkerchief, a little rice. . . . This helped me a lot. Then came the time that I married. . . . Because [now] I could think about such a thing. Because I wasn't hungry anymore.

At the close of the war, Chayale was able to go to Poland with her new husband since he was a Polish citizen, and she could take her mother with her. Gradually they worked their way to Palestine where she organized the first professional theatre in Haifa—the Haifa Yiddish Operetta Theatre—and started performing internationally. Active in the American Yiddish Theatre since her arrival in 1960, Chayale reflects on the route from the covered wagon going from shtetl to shtetl.

Every day a person who survived the war could write a book. Because in the morning it's not the same like in the middle of the day, and the night is not the same as in the morning, and the next day not the same like the day before.

From the transcript of Chayale Ash Fuhrman

14 *Lili*

With her Polish Christian classmate's identity card, Lili passed as a family member in the home of her Christian school teacher throughout the war. At the same time, her parents and brother were hidden in the home of another Christian contact, with the support of their former housekeeper. All of them, under threat of deportation and reprisal, survived.

An estimated one-third of the nine million Jews in Nazi-occupied Europe survived, some of whom were helped by Christians at great personal risk. The punishment for such a crime could be immediate death or deportation or public execution to discourage any other sympathizers from attempting such rescue. Active collaborators or greedy informants turned in neighbors, friends, even family members for a reward of brandy, sugar, or cigarettes. Such risk-taking was more common in Western Europe where liberal and democratic attitudes may have preceded Nazi takeover, and where Jews and Christians had closer social contact than in Eastern Europe. It was far more rare and dangerous in such countries as Poland which had its own history of anti-Jewish feeling, legislation, and violence.

Lili grew up in Stryj, a town in eastern Poland which is now part of the USSR. Her family was "pretty well-to-do . . . and for me life was good. I didn't dream ever of coming to America." She lived in a mixed neighborhood, had both Jewish and Christian friends, and attended a Polish school. Even after her family moved to a farm outside the town, she continued to commute to her school daily by train.

Soviet officials entered Stryj in 1939 when the Nazi-Soviet Pact divided Poland. Lili was sixteen years old.

[Immediately] the Russians came to the farm. . . . Nothing belongs to us any more because they felt that my father was a capitalist and they told him to leave everything, to give them the key, and we have to go to the city. . . . We had a big farm at that time—let's say maybe three hundred acres, horses, and cows, and a lot of people working there—but when the Russians came in, they said, "Nothing belongs to you." . . . My father had a heart attack.

Now that he was classified by the Soviet government as a capitalist farm owner, Lili's father was restricted to certain jobs in the town and felt under continuous pressure.

My father was so scared that whenever he used to come home, he used to put his finger in front of his mouth to be quiet, because he was afraid that somebody else might listen.

Lili completed her high school education in Soviet schools.

I was like in-between. . . . [On the one hand] we had to learn Russian [and] Russian history. . . . And here I hated the Russians and here they told me that whatever my father was, it wasn't right.

When the Germans took over Stryj in 1941, all of Lili's family immediately secured special working papers to try to avoid being deported.

[German] soldiers came in . . . and they took people out by buses and then to the train, and the people never came back. . . . It happened to my grandmother and uncle [and] aunt.

When we found out, people started to make . . . little bunkers—hiding places—and we had a place like that in the basement, where, through an opening from the kitchen, we went down, and we put a table on top . . . of that opening. So we were safe that way.

In 1942 . . . we had to evacuate and go to a special section [for Jews] in the city . . . required by the Germans. . . . We heard rumors that . . . a certain day the Germans are going to have a raid. [But] my father, who was going to work with my brother . . . was so sure that their papers were all right that they wouldn't hide [with us]. . . . And they walked out in the morning and he [and my brother were] taken. Of course, we did not know anything about it because we were hidden. Soon after the raid, we came up . . . from the hiding place. . . . Overnight my father came back, full of blood, with teeth knocked out. . . . He told us [that] the Germans took him . . . with my brother to a synagogue where they gathered all other Jews. Then they took them to the train station and loaded them into these cattle cars. . . . The window was closed. It was like wooden windows with nails. . . . He went to the window and tried to break it open and people were screaming, "What are you doing? . . . You are going to [endanger] all of us." He didn't listen. As soon as the train started, he pushed open the window and he threw my brother out and then he jumped after him. . . . My brother must have been then thirteen years. . . . [My father] was forty-seven years old.

We called [a Jewish] doctor to treat my father. . . . He looked at me and he says, "Why do you keep her home? . . . She doesn't look Jewish. She can pass as a non-Jew. Why don't you try to get her some papers?" My mind started working. . . .

A good friend of the family, Mrs. Belinska, was a Christian, the mother of Lili's friend from public school. She had been helping the family by selling their clothes so that they had money for food.

One day I asked her, "Do you think that your daughter would give me her birth certificate and her identification card?" At that time we had only the Russian identification card. We didn't get yet the German identification card. . . . She agreed to do it. She brought me her birth certificate and card. . . . It was with this girlfriend's picture. . . . I took my identification card, took off my picture and put it on the new identification card, and the name was Jadwiga Belinska. Then I started thinking, "Where am I going to go?"

Lili recalled some other friends who had lived near their farm.

We had a public school teacher whose husband was a high school teacher, and we knew them very well. When the Germans came, they moved away to the western part of Poland and we had their address. So I thought, What about if I go there? Maybe they will take me. . . . I didn't want to write because it would have given her too much to think. She would probably have refused. . . . My mother wouldn't let me go by myself. She asked [Mrs. Belinska] if she would travel with me. She agreed. But I asked [her], too, "When I am leaving, would you take my parents to stay with you?" . . . She took my mother to her house the same night that I was leaving and [later] my brother and my father. . . . I said good-bye to my parents.

Mrs. Belinska bought train tickets for both of them.

It was November and it was cold already. . . . We went to the station [where there were] German police in special uniforms looking for Jews. We went on the train till we came to Cracow and we had to switch the train. . . . In the waiting room . . . a German policeman approaches us. He wanted the papers. . . . He didn't see that . . . the stamp on the picture doesn't match. He didn't see that, and the funniest thing happened. He accuses that woman that she is Jewish. She says to him, "Look, my husband passed away but he . . . used to work in the

train station in Stryj. You could call there and verify it.'' And I say to the man,
''Why do you think that the lady is Jewish?'' And he says, ''Look at her. She
looks like a Jew.'' So because I was very young, I say to him, ''If you can spot
a person by the looks, well, I can say that you look Jewish, too.'' That's what
I say to him, and he lets us go.

Lili finally arrived at their friend's home in a small town near Kielce.

I knocked at the door. The lady opened, she looks at me, and she got scared.
. . . I know why she was afraid. . . . She had a small girl and she didn't want me
to say anything in front of her. . . . We walked into a separate room and . . . I
introduced the lady that brought me, and I told her that I have a birth certificate
under a different name, and I asked her if she would allow me to stay with her.
She agreed.

I stayed with them until the end of the war. They introduced me to their
friends as a cousin, [to] this lady's father-in-law . . . as her niece. . . . I started
taking care of the household and . . . I started working, knitting at home sweaters,
skirts . . . whatever, and all of the money that I made I gave them because they
didn't have much. She worked as a supervisor of a kitchen for children of poor
people . . . and he used to teach high school illegally at home. From the beginning
I used to go with them to church.

In this new city, Lili had to obtain a German ID card.

So I went to the office and I put my name ''Jadwiga Belinska'' and I read
[the application]. Were my parents Jewish? Were my grandparents Jewish? No.
And I got my identification card. . . . It was fun. . . . I outsmarted them.

By the time that I came [to this town] it was *Judenfrei*—not a single Jew
living there. At that time, they were selling Jewish furniture, Jewish clothes,
and the Poles were buying it. . . . The people that I lived with . . . didn't buy
anything.

Through Mrs. Belinska, Lillian was able to write to her family and
receive letters from them from 1942 until August 1944 when the Soviet
army occupied Poland.

[Mrs. Belinska] had my mother and my brother and my father. They stayed
hidden there. It was a small home with a little cellar. . . . We used to have a
maid at home . . . a nursemaid to my brother. She was the only one that knew
that my parents are there. [Because Mrs. Belinska] was a widow, she couldn't
hang out man's clothes, man's underwear, so this maid used to come and take
the clothes and wash them and bring them back.

I didn't hear anything about them [after the Russians took over], so after the war ended I really wasn't sure if my parents were alive. I couldn't wait to go home. I said good-bye to these people that I stayed with. The trains weren't going because the train tracks were demolished so I . . . tried to hitchhike. . . . A Russian man that was driving a Red Cross car . . . told me to lay down on the floor and he covered me . . . and I went through the . . . Russian occupied part that my parents were in.

Lili finally came to the home of the widow where her family had been hidden.

I was terribly afraid to knock at the door. Anyway I knocked and she was by herself. She says, "Your parents are alive and your brother is alive. They have their own place now. . . . I am going with you and I will go in first and I will tell them that I had regards from you. I don't want your father to get scared. . . ." It was one of the really best days of my life.

Their town was now part of Soviet territory, but because the family were still Polish citizens they were permitted to move back to Poland. They stayed in Cracow until 1946, but because there were numerous pogroms in Poland, the family went to a displaced persons' camp in Austria.

There I met for the first time concentration camp inmates. . . . It must have been a small camp and I remember seeing baby shoes, little dolls. . . . [It was not until] after the war we knew that the people didn't come back. We couldn't believe it. We thought they were taking people for labor. Even [at the time when] my father . . . broke that window and threw my brother out, people were against him because they didn't expect that something bad, really bad, is going to happen to them.

[These concentration camp survivors] wouldn't talk. I guess it was too . . . maybe they wanted to forget. Maybe they wanted to live a normal life. . . . Nobody talked about it. You knew they went through hell. . . . I saw the first time in Linz, must have been 1946 or 1947, a film about the concentration camp. I couldn't believe it was true.

In Linz, Lili worked as a typist for Simon Wiesenthal, who was head of the Jewish Identification Center, until she could emigrate to the United States. When she arrived here in 1949, she was immediately impressed.

How come they don't ask us here for passports, any identification card? Nothing? It was so different from the Russian times and the German times.

[But] still I feel a little uprooted, let's say, because my friends aren't here.

When I went to Israel for a visit, I felt at home because I met a lot of friends, school friends, and the new friends are not the same. We had common things to talk about . . . [our] young days. . . . And what I feel personally is the wartime, it really deprived me of so much. . . . There are years gone by and it's a shame because they are the nicest years of my life and they are lost. They won't come back.

From the testimony of Lillian Edelstein Steinig

15   *Marian*

When Marian was five years old, the Nazis invaded Poland. His Catholic family fled under gunfire from their ancestral homeland, and they sought refuge in Hungary with other displaced Polish families. Because they were foreigners, they were eventually deported to German work camps. During this time, Marian was continually vulnerable to the erratic decisions of the enemy and numb with fear for his family's safety. Because of the ongoing struggle to survive during his childhood, Marian suppressed his feelings and dreams until he was free to let them surface during his teen years in the United States.

The Nazi invasion of Poland on September 1, 1939, unleashed German aggression against the people of Poland as a whole. Determined to liquidate the Polish intelligentsia and wealthy landowners, and labeling the Polish people as inferior and subhuman, the Nazis uprooted millions of Poles from their homes and replaced them with "racial" Germans or Ukrainians. Indiscriminate massacres and internment eliminated millions of the "undesirables."

Marian was the second of four sons of wealthy Polish Catholic landowners. They lived in Zupanie in southeastern Poland near the borders of Hungary and the Ukraine. There were only ten such Polish Catholic families in the village and three wealthy Polish Jewish families who managed the local businesses. Most of the people were Ukrainian, who had struggled for their independence for centuries.

[The Jews and the Poles] had very good organization and relationship. Not [just] co-existence. It was more than that. [The Jews] supplied the territory with necessary things, so they were recognized as such. Poles had land. They always treasured land, like my father . . . because of his ancestors. The Ukrainians were the forgotten people. . . . There was no welfare in those days. They were not starving [but] kids would be sent out early in their life . . . to work . . . like the girl . . . that was taking care of us. I think she was sent to my parents, given by her parents, at the age of fourteen, [to see] if they would please give her a job. . . . She was our governess . . . correcting our language and manners and keeping an eye on us. . . . I think she had a very enjoyable [life with us].

There was mutual respect in this community for religious observance as well, according to Marian's earliest memories.

There was one like a rabbi. . . . He would come to visit us [around Christmas time] . . . to show us his concern for our holiday, the way I see it now. . . . I remember that he was dressed in a dark, dark hat. He was always very intelligent, very nicely spoken. . . . I remember that my parents did their utmost to [show respect to] that individual. . . . Anytime a bishop . . . would be coming to that territory, he would be representing the Jewish community [and] welcome the . . . head of the [other] religious group into the community. . . . He would be there . . . in a church . . . with [all] the religious people . . . the representative of the Jewish community . . . way up front where the bishop is. . . . He would be with them . . . the way I would like to see it.

Marian grew up with grim echoes of the First World War. When his father was twelve, his family had been held in a camp in Leipzig, Germany, where Marian's grandfather had died.

[My father] felt very guilty about the whole thing—that, as a twelve-year-old boy he should have done more than he did [to protect the family property]. Because when they came back from the camp to Poland, whatever his father had started, the neighbors took it from him [and] within a short time all of it [the lumber] was gone.

[My people were seen as] the evils of the territory. They were the Poles. Poland went through this each time there was a misunderstanding between Russia and Germany, or eastern Germany needed to expand, or needed a corridor to move through. Poland was the corridor of Europe.

In September 1939, it happened all over again. Marian was five years old.

It was one beautiful morning around ten o'clock. . . . We were in the garden playing around. I remember that my father had bees there and beehives and he told me to stay away from them [but] it was so nice to sit there observing them land on the flowers and then go back into the beehive. All of a sudden, something is flying over our head. . . . A sound that I never heard before. A big bird. Airplanes. Since we had a post office [on our estate] we had a radio, and somebody yelled out, "Hitler started a war." Those were the German planes and then there was some explosion. . . . They were using machine guns. . . . My aunt was hiding us under the trees. . . . Later on I heard stories that they were machine-gunning the cabbage patch because it looked like an organized army . . . in rows.

For two weeks . . . there was a lot of commotion and we were like being neglected. . . . Everybody was always meeting and there was a lot of talking, an awful lot of talking, and not too much time to spend with us. Everybody was always busy. Now all of a sudden my father is leaving and I couldn't tolerate it. I started banging my head against the ground, crying.

Fortunately for the family, Marian's father knew one of the officers in the Polish army unit he was attempting to join. He was told to stay home with his family since he had already served as an officer during the 1920's. Then came September 20.

Early in the morning, the dog started to bark something terrible outside. . . . He was on a chain. And then I heard some kind of yelling, screaming, and the dog didn't bark anymore. Then my mother screamed. . . . They were trying to kill my father. Now, at that time I did not know who "they" were. . . . It was Ukrainians from a different village. . . . Poles were killing Ukrainians in *their* territory, so they came to revenge that act and stir up the rest of the Ukrainians to do the same.

They killed the dog and . . . one of the leaders lifted the cane to hit my father. . . . The cane had a sharp metal tip on the end, very sharp. . . . He was going to smash [my father] on the head. . . . My mother ran out and screamed, "You have to kill me first!" . . . Well, then there was an awful lot of excitement. The guy in charge of our post office was Ukrainian. They were all Ukrainians [on our land]. He jumped in and he grabbed the cane and said, "I am in charge here. I have the keys. I have the weapons. You talk to me." Then he whispered in my parents' ear, "Run because all they are looking for is the taste of blood, and then nobody will be able to stop them."

That was six in the morning. My youngest brother was just two weeks old so my mother was just after delivery. . . . My younger brother didn't even have his shoes on. . . . Nobody had a chance to put them on . . . there was so much commotion. . . . We ran towards the Hungarian border to run away from this. It was in the fall . . . after the wheat was cut down . . . and those jaggedy things were sticking up. My younger brother's feet started to bleed so [somebody] had to carry him. My mother was carrying the youngest.

Two Ukrainians ran after us . . . shooting in the woods. . . . Finally they realized that we would get away. . . . When I looked back, the flag, the Polish flag on the barracks of the border patrol, was being broken off. . . . They had horses. It was just like cowboys. They attached a rope to it and they started pulling.

[My parents had been] constantly told by the government that we are ready and able to stop any aggression from Hitler's side because Hitler was making a lot of noises and the world knew it. . . . We were told we have it [preparation for the invasion]. They would take an airplane and a new machine gun and they would drive it from place to place and show the people . . . and it would be the same airplane and weapon that would travel from city to city, from village to village, just to keep the people confused that things are fine. . . . They were, I think, double-crossed by the government. They were now aware of what's going to happen. . . . That is the sad thing. . . . It's a betrayal.

Once in Hungary, Marian's family joined other Polish nationals who had escaped the Nazi takeover of Poland. The Hungarian government permitted clusters of Poles to live and work in different locations until supplies and jobs ran short. Then they would be moved to other "camps." For almost five years, Marian and his family moved from camp to camp, in one town grouped in private homes, in another housed in military barracks. Educated members of the refugee community tutored the children, an attempt to stabilize their isolated and insecure lives.

The Hungarians were not too friendly to us. They wanted to stay neutral, I think. . . . We were always kept an eye on. We were the foreigners. We were the unwanted ones.

Though Marian's father had not been politically active in Poland, in exile he became very involved.

My parents had to report . . . to police stations [regularly] . . . but perhaps it was only . . . because my father was organizing an underground movement in Hungary. . . . What we were doing was actually making artificial passports and smuggling young men through Hungary to Romania . . . to wherever they had to go to fight the Germans. . . . There were young [Christian] Polish men and there were also young Jews. . . . All Polish citizens. . . . [My father] was traveling constantly to Budapest . . . the Hungarian capital, and wherever we were, he was on the go. . . . [Despite his feelings of betrayal by the Polish government, he told us] our duty was from then on to fight Hitler with everything we have.

Now, he had a family. I don't know whether I could do that, to give up on my kids and my wife and go ahead and spend all the time on the road knowing if I would be caught, their lives would be in danger.

Since Marian's father was supposed to be working in the camp and to report to the local police station on a regular basis, there were times when his mother would ask a cousin to sign her husband's name in his absence.

They discovered that somebody else was signing and that is what kicked us out of the one place to another. I think that was the reason. I am not sure what made us move so much. . . . [Children] were excluded from all serious talks. . . . They had their own place. . . .

We had a lot of parties. . . . I remember all those big people coming, with big degrees. There was an awful lot of intelligentsia that left Poland . . . educated individuals who could care less about their wealth. They just took off with their lives. They would always gather and it seemed like a party, but now I understand that those were political meetings.

Marian's family received word about the fate of their village through a Jewish neighbor who caught up with them in Hungary.

When things got very rough in Poland . . . he went to our priest . . . and asked him for our baptismal certificates. . . . When the war started . . . my parents had [told] the priest if somebody needs it, give them our certificates. . . . We didn't need any . . . but Jews would need the papers. . . . [Our Jewish neighbor] traveled and met us in . . . Hungary with that birth certificate.

[He told us that] they picked [one July 4]—like a Fourth of July celebration— to kill off Jews. I think . . . a movement . . . of Ukrainians in that territory . . . was organized by Hitler . . . prior to the war. . . . They were given authority to clean out the territory and it will be theirs. . . . [Our neighbor's] wife, for some reason, went outside and they shot her. . . . His mother . . . went out to help her daughter-in-law and she was also killed. . . . One Jewish girl took a refuge in a Ukrainian house. She took their name, she took their religion, and she took their garments. She would go to the Orthodox Church with them. On [that] July fourth . . . they took her out of the church . . . and walked her so many kilometers to kill her with the rest of the group. . . . The family [that was sheltering her] was not able to stop it. . . . It was a mass movement. . . . It was like a deportation, to remove them from the territory . . . because otherwise the word would get out [about the massacre]. . . . They [thought they] were just being moved from one place to another and then something happened in the meantime and they were removed from this earth.

Marian's great-uncle, who had stayed behind in Poland, also witnessed the violence.

It was quite late . . . and he heard shots. He saw horses driving around one of the Polish homes and shooting at the house and then they set fire to the house. People tried to escape the house and they were shot right there. Then they would go to the next house and again surround and start shooting anybody that tried to escape and burn the house down.

[Another night he] hid in the cemetery behind a tombstone. The cemetery was not far from the home where I was born. And they observed all this terrible thing going on. One family had five daughters. . . . They lined them up, father, mother, oldest daughter to the youngest. They took out . . . an ax plus the wooden block. They would lay the kids on the block and chop the heads off. Everybody would scream. They would faint and they would bring them back to it, pour water on them, and do the next execution. They killed them all like that, the whole family and then they burned their house. . . . A Polish family killed by Ukrainians. . . . They were not political people, but they had rights to the territory. . . . [They thought] if they cleaned that territory that it's theirs. Of course, it was false belief on their side. Later on, Hitler got even with them. He wanted people to work for him, but don't organize on your own.

Although they had escaped such massacres in their homeland, the Polish exiles in Hungary faced prejudice and, eventually, persecution.

[To the Hungarian Nazis] Poles . . . were lower than the dirt. We were the enemies of the state . . . of the German nation. I was always questioning myself, Why am I evil? Why am I hated? . . . Ever since Hitler went through Hungary [to fight the Russians] we experienced nothing but . . . fear. It was in the air. . . . [They used] a very dirty word . . . derogatory . . . [about the Poles] with a meaning that "we will get you."

It was a precarious existence that they shared with the Hungarian Jewish population before 1944.

Across a big empty yard, there was a Jewish family. . . . There were younger girls, two girls. . . . It was a blessing to us that we were allowed to play with them because we were actually nobodies in a new territory. Hungarian boys we had trouble with because we had to fight all the time. . . . They didn't want us around.

Then, all of a sudden, I noticed yellow stars. . . . The places that we go to buy food, we noticed [the Jewish shopkeepers] have a star on themselves, but still they did not know what is in store for them. . . . If you did that to me, I would try to sneak out. . . . [But] I am thinking that now. At that time I just questioned why.

First the Jews were restricted to a ghetto. Marian's mother wanted to take her children's two Jewish playmates but she could not.

The uproar was such [from] the Polish community. "Do you know what you are doing to us? Not to yourself. Do you think about us?" And also, "How do you know whether this will be better for [them]?" . . . Nobody knew actually that they were going to be destroyed. . . . [But] I don't think that they kept Jews in the ghetto more than two weeks. . . . They were transported.

From that moment everybody [among the Polish refugees] was so afraid. We were afraid to go out on the street and afraid to say something and you always looked back [to see] who was walking behind you.

In this ominous climate, Marian and his Polish friends tried to protect themselves.

We would go to church. I was an altar boy—the Hungarians didn't like us but the priests did. For some reason, we were more kind. . . . Knowing that everybody hates you, you become extremely kind . . . extremely shy . . . not as arrogant as some of those other boys. . . . You had to be extremely kind to everybody . . . to survive.

I remember twice or three times, a single [German] soldier walked in the church. . . . Perhaps he had a family in Germany that he thought greatly of. But yet we didn't mean anything [to him]. . . . We feared him in the church when he walked in because that was a deadly force that walked in—a force that had all the rights to life and death. It was all up to him. Nobody else. No courts. He could decide right on the spot. . . . I lifted my head to God and said, "God, why can't he be nicer to us when he leaves this house?"

In the fall of 1944, after the Gypsies and Jews had been deported, it was the Poles' turn.

They came from one house to another and they arrested everybody in the house, took them out on the street and walked us under guard to the next house where the Poles lived so you could not give signals or anything. . . . Those were the German soldiers and Hungarians. Both. The Hungarians, I guess, knew where we lived, and the Germans made sure that it was done. When they put us into that place though . . . one big mansion . . . it was only German soldiers that guarded us. They did not trust, maybe, Hungarians. Perhaps they felt that some Hungarians were too friendly with us prior to this.

I remember my [Hungarian] friend Lotsie. We lived in the same building. . . . He was a very good friend. . . . As a matter of fact, we spent more time in his place than ours. When my parents needed [something] they always went down [to Lotsie's family's apartment]. When they took us into that [which] I call a prison one morning, I saw Lotsie at the fence. It was all fenced in iron. . . . I went up to him. "Lotsie!" And he went away from the fence before I got there. I'm sure he cried when he went away that he was not allowed to have any dealing with us. At that time I didn't understand, but it hurt so much. It hurt so much that my best friend, my best friend in the whole world, would not speak to me anymore. He ran away. From that time I never saw him anymore.

Shortly after this, the Polish population of the town was deported to work camps in Germany. Knowing that Soviet troops were approaching the town, Marian's parents felt that this fate was the better of two evils.

I believe that they trusted the Germans more than they trusted the Russians. I believe that they felt the Germans were more intelligent individuals, more civilized than the eastern Russian hordes. There were terrible stories about Russians from the First World War.

Marian was eleven-years-old. His older brother was twelve, his younger brothers ten and five, when they were deported on December 31, 1944.

So now comes this moment of leaving. . . . We are trying to take everything dearest to us with us. The dearest thing that I had was a stamp collection. A lot of those stamps were the latest stamps of Hitler, the latest issues of Hitler, but, yet, as a stamp collector, to me, it meant a treasure because I had a full set of each issue and they were beautiful. Hitler stamps were large and colorful . . . like an inch and a half by two inches. . . . The other stamps were not as pretty. . . . I had all kinds of stamps—Hungarian stamps and French stamps and English stamps—and I was exchanging them with Hungarian boys who collected stamps. . . . It was a big hobby and it was something that we got deeply involved in. So I had these two or three books of stamps and I was carrying them under my arms and this German soldier kicked me and the stamps fell out of the books from under my arm. So I started grabbing them, and he put his foot on them. . . . I grabbed some from under his foot. Big foot, big boots. Winter time. And I started tearing up the stamp collection, crying, and tearing it up. . . . For some reason, that was the most important thing to me at that moment. . . . I didn't want him—them—to have my treasure. . . . If I can't have it, I will not allow you to enjoy my pleasure. And I felt good.
We walked . . . maybe three and a half kilometers, one and a half miles to the railroad station. . . . We just had to carry and drag whatever we had. . . . It wasn't too bad on snow. . . . All helmets and uniforms and boots and a lot of guns. . . . There was no more civilian life. . . . Empty railroad cars, animal cars, with open doors and us. . . . If I remember, there were . . . around six cars . . . seventy-nine people in our wagon, packed like sardines. They slammed the door shut. It was a sliding-type door and they put the kind of lock . . . with wire and lead so nobody

could open the wagons. It was probably like two-thirty or three o'clock in the afternoon. They did not feed us that day.... They locked us in that train and we stayed there till midnight. I remember the whistles, the sirens, welcoming New Year's Eve. New Year's and we were all in a cage already.

Just waiting. All those hours, cold, windy, but then it got worse because the wind started to whistle. And the people started to sing. They started to do different things to occupy their minds. And I remember that the men were yelling out every so often to change place.... At that time, I didn't realize what they were doing, but they were changing places on the outside against the wall [where] there were big cracks in the wagon.... First he was facing the outside ... and then he had to turn around ... move in and the next groups would take the outside line because they realized that [otherwise] they would all freeze. Constantly they had to move their feet.... Boom, boom, boom, boom. Everybody was marching some place and yet you couldn't lift your feet high.... because you were hitting the next person.... There was an awful lot of horse manure on the floor of the wagon.... I heard the adults say that that's what saved our lives. Horse manure ... was insulation.

For three days they traveled in the sealed trains without stopping.

The first stop ... must have been in the morning because I can remember the sun coming out, shining over the ... valleys. They allowed us to make a circle and take care of our needs as human beings, to urinate, etc. It was very cold. I know we were huddling [close to] my mother and not knowing what to do. We never did anything like that in the presence of other people, surrounded by people with guns around. The circle was small.... And I remember just one old lady, she was saying to my mother, "How can I?" She also had a very big title.... I think a judge's wife.... This group was mostly old women and, of course, women with children, wives that had been left behind because their husbands had already left, and other, intelligent people, people that had position [and] big titles.... And my mother said, "Just lift your skirt and don't worry about it. We are in a cage now. We are no longer humans."

By the fourth day they reached Vienna and while under guard on the train platform, Marian and his brother decided to take certain matters into their own hands.

I and my older brother ... were messengers in Hungary for my father. Whatever messages he wanted to send, political messages, signals from him to his subordinates, he would use us and we would deliver the messages.... We were very strongly taught that we are Poles and we owe our country our lives, so whatever we did to destroy the enemy, we must remember that we are Poles.

So in Vienna, we saw the express trains for the first time in our lives ... full of German brass, soldiers in the windows. . . . Somehow we got away, me and my brother, far enough that we found a piece of railroad track . . . about four feet . . . in length and we went and put it across the railroad track on one side, propped it up with rocks and ran back to our group, to our parents, and we said, "Do you know what we did? The next train that comes through here it's going to go off. We put a piece of steel across the tracks." And my mother said, "Do you know what you did? We are all dead because as soon as the train goes off, . . . the soldiers . . . will shoot us immediately." We had to sneak back, crawl back . . . pull and jerk this thing out and it was a heavy thing, and within seconds . . . the train comes through. We were very happy that we did something wonderful but it was actually something very stupid.

The trainload of prisoners was taken to Strasshof, just outside of Vienna, where they were greeted by Ukrainian guards who were, coincidentally, from their district in Poland. Immediately the guards recognized the police chief and assistant police chief among the Polish prisoners and called them out of line. The police chief returned six hours later, holding his beaten head, his teeth knocked out. His assistant never returned. Marian's family learned that he had once arrested one of these Ukrainian guards for stealing a pig. When the Germans occupied the territory, they had released all the prisoners in the Polish jails, including this guard.

All the prisoners got a rank of some sort [from the Germans] and [were told], "You know what to get. Go and get them" . . . those people who were in charge . . . the people they hated. [The assistant police chief] was one of them.

Now each Polish prisoner was issued a diamond-shaped patch—a yellow P on a blue background, ironically the colors of the Ukrainian flag rather than the red and white of Poland. Marian's family was assigned to a work camp in Wilhelmshaven, near Berlin, where better food, pillows, and sheets provided a model image to curious officials from Berlin. The reality of the camp was a nightmarish interrogation of the prisoners to expose Polish underground and other enemies of the Reich.

[But then] one day came the big bombing of Berlin. What a sight and what a sound! We were [hidden in a bunker] but we were only thirty kilometers from Berlin and that bombing lasted like four or four and a half hours. . . . For three days or more after the bombing, Berlin was on fire and money was coming down even into our camp—the German marks—but they were all burned. . . . Banks were hit, I think, and the heat took them up in the air and the wind threw them around. Tremendous heat. . . . We were tremendously scared but so eagerly happy.

From Wilhelmshaven to Bayreuth to Neumarkt, the family moved to camps filled with refugees all "trying not to be labeled as political . . . Poles . . . Russians . . . French . . . They were captured civilians . . . that [the Germans] could not trust."

In [Neumarkt] I was a woman. . . . Men were men and any male below twelve was a woman and went to work with the women. . . . I felt very bad . . . that I am something not right. I can't go with my brother and I can't stick with my father. . . . I understand that I am not quite twelve but I am the same size as my brother. I am capable of doing the same thing. . . . [But] I am forced to be with my mother and I don't know . . . I just felt that I don't fit into this world's puzzle. Like there is something wrong with me.

Marian worked alongside his mother under heavy guard, gathering loads of wood on their backs in the freezing forests. One day, his sockless feet started to freeze and his mother urged him to take off his shoes and rub his feet with the snow. As Marian began to lose all feeling in his feet, his mother dropped her load of wood and started rubbing his feet, tearing off part of her dress to wrap them. Suddenly an air raid forced them into a ditch, knee deep with mud, and Marian's mother urged him to run for the barracks. Kept in the ditch by the siren's command, the frustrated Ukrainian guard hurled his stick at Marian "like they used to get rabbits" but Marian was able to crawl to safety. He can remember no punishment.

The worst thing that I would get was a good kick. And then you would fly. . . . For some reason I never cried . . . or showed anything that would make my parents' day worse. I never asked for food or anything. . . . I guess we would always feel it. [Long pause] You try not to [show it] knowing that . . . by doing so you hurt your parents . . . more. You were trying to be a super adult and it's unreal. It's hard to become an adult at such an early age. . . . [Now] I am very conscious of somebody being young and enjoying it, but I don't really know what it is. To be honest, I don't miss that. I don't think I miss it. I want somebody else to have it.

There was no such thing [then] as playing. . . . Not even making a ball out of a rag or something. . . . It wasn't to be. Nobody even tried because I think that everybody sensed and felt and knew the terrible thing we were in. And you tried to pitch in and not make it any worse.

Later on when I became, I guess, twelve . . . I was allowed to go with my brother to clean out after the bombing. The men would be sent to town to clean up the place and take unexploded bombs . . . dig a hole . . . and try to put them in carefully, slowly. . . . You walk to town, you walk back. . . . My father would say . . . break away. . . . "Try the butcher shop and maybe he will sell you some bones." . . . We had money . . . and as a kid it was no big deal because kids are sneaks . . . and [the guards] never pay attention too much. . . . The adults they watch.

The brothers would alternate running into a butcher shop so it would not look as if they were together. Then they would mess up their hair, take off their jackets, and pretend to be two other boys, store after store, time after time, until the shopowners would yell, "Enough!" It was only in the last two months of Marian's imprisonment that he could live on the men's side.

[By then] there was no feeling anymore. . . . There was no transition. No big deal. Except I knew now my responsibility was to get something for the family. To bring something in. To cheat as much as I can. To sneak away from the work force and to buy something to eat. We had money . . . changed into German marks . . . but we used that money instead of toilet paper just to get even. . . . We used it because we didn't want them to get it. . . . To use that and just destroy it. . . . It gave us a tremendous feeling.

These were their chances to escape, to just keep on going while sneaking away from the work detail for food. But this was not part of Marian's dream.

Never. You had something very dear left behind and the only thing you could do is think how to free them. There was no way. . . . It was a tough situation that you were in. Say you could run away—where would you go?

Coming from a religious Catholic background, Marian still gets depressed around Christmas and Easter, recalling a single religious service in the camps.

It was Easter . . . in one of their garages. I remember . . . Hitler's portrait, very high, a very big one, and underneath they had some kind of table, altar. Ukrainian Orthodox monks were all around it. They dressed differently and they were singing to Hitler, praying to Hitler, but mentioning God . . . to help Hitler and the whole German nation.

[As for any other Christian observance] it never happened. On the trains I remember that they were singing religious songs, never political, just religious, to keep them alive because it was cold. Just to get everybody involved, I guess. . . . Not to give up. Later on, as soon as we reached the camps, they removed all that. Nobody ever talked. Period.

[Personal religion] is the only thing that helped us survive. Hoping that there is a miracle around the corner. That something will happen. [That] this cannot be allowed.

For some reason we could communicate by just looking at each other, into the eyes, and we all thought about the same thing—that perhaps tomorrow will change. Things will change. But we did not say it out loud. . . . Me and my brothers and my parents. We would try to catch each other's eye, which was very sad. Once you are in that type of situation it is so sad that just the glimpse of somebody's eye tells you the whole story. . . . The real intimate feeling of sharing . . . of love . . . was not allowed to be expressed . . . but kindness and sharing there was. I remember it was throughout the whole system. If somebody was unable to walk, everybody would try to help him because soon as he fell, that was the end of it. . . . It was mutual because, I guess, they all knew they were in the same boat. There is no way out.

Marian and his family were liberated from Neumarkt in May 1945 and lived in a series of DP camps before they emigrated to the United States in 1949. Only twelve when he was liberated, Marian asks himself now why he had so few thoughts, dreams, or fantasies while he was in the camp.

I believe what happens once you are reduced to that level, you don't have any dreams. You don't recall anything. You just are where you are. . . . The dehumanization did play the major part in it. They removed this beautiful human dream, of growing up to be somebody and to live up to your parents' dreams. . . . Then it was also painful to go back . . . to play around with something you had before. Something that gave you pleasure. But, also, there was a third factor involved—that we were not given the opportunity, the chance, to actually think. That was taken. . . . You were yelled at . . . you were pushed . . . you were moved. . . . They constantly kept you disturbed and ducking. . . . I don't remember ever dreaming. . . . Maybe it's the . . . mind that locks everything away. To keep you from losing whatever you have. . . . It is so easy for a child to lose his mind altogether if [he permits himself] to realize and compare.

[Dreams began] when I came here. I believe that I experienced a total relaxation and freedom. My dream of life was to own a gun. A gun meant life. . . . My wish, my desire, was to put my hand on a gun . . . because a gun meant so much when I was in captivity . . . power . . . freedom . . . everything. So as soon as I had a chance I bought a weapon to go hunting. . . . Then I went into the [American] military . . . the 82nd Airborne and I bought a .45 pistol as soon as I came out. . . . Like a child with a new toy. . . . I had to take it apart and I had to oil it and pretend that I am looking at the barrel. . . . That feeling was for quite a while because as soon as I had the weapons, it rekindled the old memories.

I always would wake up in the middle of the night. The Germans were after me. They were chasing me and I was running away and it is so hard when you are asleep to run. They are getting closer and your legs are so tired. You can't move. You can't run because of blankets or whatever you have over you. And they are getting closer and closer and, finally, you wake up. . . . When I got the .45 . . . the dreams would change that Germans are not just chasing me, but if I could only get to my gun . . . and to get even with them . . . things will change. . . . I never reached the pistol. . . . Never. I was always trying so hard, so terribly hard to get to it, and I never got to it.

Finally, it left me. I am free. I don't have to have a weapon. . . . I think I just loosened up a little bit. I started having more fun and found out more about women. . . . I was very shy prior to that. I never had a chance to play my role as a growing-up boy. . . . I started to become human again.

From the testimony of Marian Turzanski

Index

About the Editor

JOSEY G. FISHER is Director, Holocaust Oral History Archive of Gratz College, and a practicing clinical social worker.